Tracking God in Your Life

Books by Laurie Polich Short

40 Verses to Ignite Your Faith

Faith, Doubt, and God's Mysterious Timing

Tracking God in Your Life

When Changing Nothing Changes Everything

Finding Faith in the Dark

Grace-Filled Stepparenting

Tracking God in Your Life

How to See God's Work in Your Past,
Experience His Presence,
and Trust Him with Your Future

LAURIE POLICH SHORT

BETHANYHOUSE
a division of Baker Publishing Group
Minneapolis, Minnesota

© 2026 by Laurie Polich Short

Published by Bethany House Publishers
Minneapolis, Minnesota
BethanyHouse.com

Bethany House Publishers is a division of
Baker Publishing Group, Grand Rapids, Michigan

Printed in the United States of America

Library of Congress Cataloging-in-Publication Data
Names: Polich-Short, Laurie, author.
Title: Tracking God in your life : how to see God's work in your past, experience his presence, and trust him with your future / Laurie Polich Short.
Description: Minneapolis, Minnesota : Bethany House, a division of Baker Publishing Group, [2026] | Includes bibliographical references.
Identifiers: LCCN 2025016495 | ISBN 9780764244926 (paperback) | ISBN 9780764246180 (casebound) | ISBN 9781493452590 (ebook)
Subjects: LCSH: Providence and government of God—Christianity. | Trust in God—Christianity. | God (Christianity) | Christian life—Biblical teaching.
Classification: LCC BT135 .P579 2026 | DDC 231/.5—dc23/eng/20250821
LC record available at https://lccn.loc.gov/2025016495

Some names and recognizable details have been changed to protect the privacy of those who have shared their stories for this book.

Cover design by Derek Thornton / Notch Design

The author is represented by WordServe Literary Group, WordServeLiterary.com.

Baker Publishing Group publications use paper produced from sustainable forestry practices and postconsumer waste whenever possible.

26 27 28 29 30 31 32   7 6 5 4 3 2 1

To those who've glimpsed an outline
of a footprint pressing in from the other side.
I hope this will help you color it in.

Contents

Introduction

This is a book you will participate in. It will be an opportunity for you to track God in the circumstances and events of your life. My hope is that when you are through, you'll be able to more clearly recognize where God is in the circumstances you are living right now.

Maybe you've seen glimpses of God's presence but have never documented it. Or you don't know whether you've seen any evidence of God at all. But I'm going to assume that because you picked up this book, you would like to be able to see God's movement in your life.

In the chapters that follow, you will be introduced to eight ways to look for God's presence. I will give you some examples from other people's experiences to show you different ways to look for God in the events and circumstances that have happened in your life. You will look at the doors that have opened and closed, how you ended up in different places than you planned, the difficulties you've endured and how those difficulties were used, and the unexpected people who were brought into your life. Through reflective questions and prompts, you will be invited to look more closely at these things, and I believe that behind them, you will see the presence of God.

Tracking God builds your faith. It is a practice that started in the Old Testament: When the Israelites realized God had been with them, they made an altar by piling stones. Because they left their stones behind as evidence of God's presence, they could return to them when they felt anxious and alone. When other people saw a pile of stones, they knew God had shown up in that place. These stone altars reminded people that the same God who showed up in that place would be with them, no matter what they faced.

You can think of this book as your pile of stones.

For years as an author and speaker, I've been helping people discover spiritual insights about God and have used many illustrations from my life that point to God's presence. The eight practices in these chapters will help you find God's presence in *your* story, and your findings will be included in what the pages hold. The questions, Scriptures, and stories will inspire you to personally reflect on and piece together the story of God in your life.

So get out your favorite pen and take your time through this book. I hope it will help you to realize that you have more of God's attention than you might have thought. He has been weaving the events and circumstances of your life together in more ways than you've been aware of. Your discoveries will reveal those ways.

one

Footprints

Tracking is the process of interpreting signs that reveal where someone or something has been, in hopes of discovering where they might be. That is a pretty good description of what you are about to do with God.

When you are tracking an animal or a person, you usually begin by looking for footprints. Since God is invisible, the footprints that belong to God need to be seen by using more than your eyes. Before you think I'm being too mystical, consider some other invisible things you observe without using your eyes: the air you breathe, for instance, or the wind blowing on your face. You don't question that those things are there, but you can't see them. Tracking God is similar to tracking those things. The way you see them is by observing their effects.

There are also other senses we use to track invisible things. We hear a voice in the dark and know that a certain person is there, even if we don't see them. We are prompted to action by a thought, and that is enough evidence that the thought happened—even if we didn't see that thought with our eyes.

I hope this book will help you open your senses to some things that are not clearly discernible to the eye, so they have to be looked at differently. Like the upper footprint on the cover of this book—a closer look at the shadows and lines shows that it is pressing in from the other side. God's footprints may have been in front of you all along, but you might never have taken the time to notice them.

You may never have pieced together your story with God in the timing of events and circumstances that have happened—or looked at what God did down the road with the difficulties and disappointments you've experienced. As you look back over your life, you will make connections between things that happened to you and around you that you've never considered before. When you do this, I believe you will see the hand of God.

Through each chapter, you will be led to look for God from a different angle, prompted by stories of people who experienced God in that particular way. When you finish the book, you will know what to look for to see God more expansively in your life. Learning to track God's presence gives you perseverance when you are in a long wait, confidence when you can't see what is happening, comfort when you feel alone, and trust when the thing you want is eluding you.

And since tracking usually begins with looking for footprints, that's where we will begin. The irony of "tracking God" is that you discover a God who has been tracking you. God has been with you even when you were not aware of His presence.

A poem titled "Footprints in the Sand"[1] has been published in various forms, but the first one I ever saw was embossed on a bookmark. It recounted a man's dream of looking back at his life by examining a long stretch of beach and observing the footprints. He is looking for where God was accompanying him by searching for a second set of footprints next to his own. Where the man sees two sets of footprints, he concludes that God was with him. Where he sees only one set of footprints, he assumes he was alone. He notices that those were the most difficult and painful times in his life.

The man cries out, asking God why He abandoned him during his worst moments. The perspective shift happens when God replies that those were the times when He carried him.[2]

I always appreciated a comic strip loosely based on this poem that included a skid mark in the sand. God says, "And that long groove over there is when I dragged you kicking and screaming."[3]

Whether or not this groove speaks to your life like it does mine, the image of God's footprints being less obvious in certain seasons offers a good starting point for tracking God's presence in places you never thought to look. And in case you fear that you won't see much evidence of God in your life because of things you've done that God didn't like, I thought it would be good to begin with the story of a man who was a deceiver and a liar when he first saw God. A closer look at Jacob's first encounter with God reveals something important about the way God shows up in our lives.

God Goes First

It's a mystical scene in Genesis 28 when Jacob lies down to rest and has a vivid dream in which God visits him. Prior to this, Jacob had deceived his twin brother and stolen his birthright, and he had run away from home because of the fury he caused in his family. Yet Jacob receives not just a visit but also a blessing from God. In Jacob's dream there is a long stairway, with angels ascending and descending, and the Lord appears at the top of the stairway. He says he will bless Jacob and his descendants and watch over him wherever he goes (v. 15). When Jacob wakes up, he proclaims these words (v. 16):

"Surely the LORD is in this place, and I was not aware of it."

Jacob's words indicate that he felt God's presence in a way he hadn't experienced before. But the important thing to notice is that before Jacob did anything to deserve it, God blessed him first. When Jacob looked back at some of the details of his dream, he realized God had used the dream to make His presence known to him. Looking back at some of your first experiences with God will help you remember the places God made His presence known to you. This is your starting point for tracking God in your life.

Think back on the first time you remember being aware of God—maybe it was when you looked up at the sky and saw a million stars or watched a sunrise. It could have been when you received an answer to a prayer, or a time when you unexpectedly felt something in church. You may never remember *not* being aware of God. But I want you to try to think about *your first experience* of having a "God awareness."

Begin your reflections by jotting down some notes on the next page. (This is the time to grab that pen if you haven't yet.) Where did your first God awareness happen? How old were you? What happened? Write down any details you remember. This is only the beginning of your reflections, so don't worry about being exhaustive.

Another way to track God's footprints is by reflecting on when you might have felt prompted to respond to God. After Jacob had his encounter with God, he made a vow to give God his devotion and a tenth of his resources as a response to God blessing him. Your response to God may be a number of things—a decision to get baptized, a time you stood up or raised your hand in a service, the first time you took communion, or a prayer you said inviting God to have your heart. There are many ways to respond to God, so write down anything that comes to mind.

What's interesting to note about the timing of Jacob's encounter with God is that it happened after he stole his brother's birthright, so God did not show up as a reward for something Jacob did for Him. God comes to us before we come to God. We see God also doing that in Genesis 16, in the story of Hagar. After Hagar runs away because she is being mistreated, God meets her in the desert, and Hagar's response indicates that God sees her first. She says, "I have now seen the One who sees me" (v. 13).

Looking back on when you first experienced God's presence, is there anything that makes you think that God might have initiated the encounter? If so, what?

Reflecting on Hagar's statement, have you ever felt seen by God? Maybe by receiving unexpected comfort in a difficult time, or when something happened that gave you the feeling you weren't alone? YES / NO

When my cousin's husband died at home after a long battle with cancer, she looked outside to her roof and saw that a cross had formed from the lights in the sky. The timing of seeing this image at the moment her husband passed made her aware of God's presence with her during that dark time.

As you think back on times when you felt sad or alone, have you ever felt watched or cared for by God? If so, what was it that made you feel that way?

Another angle on tracking God's footprints in your life is to think about how God has placed people around you who positioned you to see and experience His presence. Jacob's father, Isaac, and his grandfather, Abraham, both had vibrant relationships with God, so Jacob was exposed to God's presence before he encountered God himself.

Many times, these people who expose you to God are close to you, but sometimes people come into your life and point you to God without knowing they've done so. I had a brief three-week dating relationship in high school (the average length of most of my high school relationships) that happened to fall during the timing of a Young Life weekend camp, which I never would have gone to if I wasn't with that boy. It was there I heard for the first time that God loved me and wanted a relationship with me, and that set a course for my faith.

As you look back, can you think of anyone God may have placed in your life to point you to His presence? Someone in your family, or a friend? Perhaps it was someone who invited you to church, or showed you something in the Bible, or shared their faith with you? Maybe it was someone who prayed for you? Write down any name or names that come to mind.

Seeing purpose behind the things that happen in your life is part of how you track God's presence. It's how you know God is pursuing you before you pursue Him because you can see how He orchestrated some things in your life. This is not only true with people God has placed around you, but also in your circumstances when God does something, or prevents something, in your life. We don't always see the good in what God is doing while He is doing it. Sometimes we feel like the man being dragged kicking and screaming in the comic strip, and we might even feel that God is being mean. But your judgment of how things look while they are happening may change when you watch what continues to happen. That's the benefit of looking back at the whole story—you can see how the story evolved.

Because God has a broader perspective than you do, your view of what God does often ends up changing. The plan you had that didn't work out may eventually reveal evidence of God's care. We'll explore this a lot more in the chapters to come, but pause here and write down the first time you remember something happening in your life that was *not* what you wanted to happen.

What was it?

Has anything transpired in your life since that has changed your perspective on what happened? YES / NO

If so, what?

When God works in a way that is different from what you wanted, it generally provokes one of two responses: You either move away from God or end up growing in your faith. Tracking God's presence involves not only looking at what God has done, but also at how you have changed. When you evolve from believing that God is only good when He gives you what you want into understanding that God sometimes gives you what others need, you will inevitably see and experience more of God.

Signs of a Growing Faith

Looking back at the ways God has been at work in your story, you can find God in things that happened to cause your faith to grow and mature. We see this growth in the story of Leah in Genesis 29.

Leah's story begins in an unfortunate way: She was given away by her father to a groom who didn't want her. Not only that, at her wedding celebration, her groom thought he was marrying someone else. The groom was Jacob, and he had made an agreement with Leah's dad, Laban, to marry Leah's younger sister Rachel. However, on the day of the wedding, Laban replaced Rachel with Leah because he wanted his eldest daughter to marry first. Because of the veil on Leah's face (and probably a lot of wine), Jacob doesn't realize he's marrying the wrong woman until the next morning. So Leah's first morning as a bride begins with Jacob's disappointed face, which (I'm guessing) was not the start to a marriage she dreamed she would one day have.

Laban appeases Jacob by telling him that if he works for him seven more years, he will be able to marry Rachel too. So Leah's entire married life is marked by being second best. We don't get a chance to hear Leah's thoughts until she begins to have children. But if you look at how she names her four sons in Genesis 29:31–35, you can observe a progression in Leah's faith.

When she names her first son Reuben, she says, "Surely my husband will love me now" (v. 32); with Simeon, she says, "The Lord heard that I am not loved" (v. 33); and with Levi, she says, "Now at last my husband will become attached to me" (v. 34). In the naming of her first three children, it's not hard to see how jealousy and longing consumed Leah's heart. However, when her fourth son is born, you can observe a shift in Leah: She declares, "This time I will praise the Lord" and names him Judah (v. 35).

Leah's progression of faith is represented through the names of her children. This is how we observe God's growing presence in her life. Sometimes when we look back, it is in similarly subtle ways that we can see God's growing presence in our life.

So, this is a chance for you to think back on your spiritual growth. Have you changed or altered any attitude or behavior since you first believed in or responded to God? In what way(s) is your life different because of your relationship with God? Would you say you have grown in your faith or stayed the same? If you can think of any markers of growth that you observe in your life since you started believing in God, write them below.

The final question for you to think about in this chapter is what we see in Leah's life through her son Judah: She came to the place where she shifted her focus from what she wanted and didn't have to what God *was* doing for her instead. Have you ever had this kind of shift in your relationship with God—when you were able to let go of something you wanted and trust God for what He was doing in your life? YES / NO

If so, what happened? If not, how would such a shift change your current faith? Reflect on this below.

In the story of Leah's marriage, she never got what she wanted. But in God's bigger story, Leah was given an honored role. Leah's son, Judah, is the one who carries the family line to Christ. (See Matthew 1:2–16.) The way Leah names Judah represents what God desires for all of us—that we stop fixating on what we think will satisfy us and trust the One who holds our lives.

It seems that God's longing is to walk with us—and sometimes carry us—to our own "Judah naming" experiences. It's not easy to get to that place if you've had to lay aside something you've dreamed of, longed for, or begged God to do. That is when you need to pause in between the lines we're given of Leah's story to imagine her painful process, and realize that her journey is more than you read.

Rachel may have had her husband's love, but she experienced great pain (and even death) in childbirth. Loss touches all our lives; it just comes in different packages. Ironically, loss is also one of the places where God shows up most profoundly, and you will see that in a future chapter.

As you track the ways that God has been at work in your past, you will learn how to watch for where God is right now, which is sometimes different from where you are looking. The image of a single set of footprints in the sand showcases that truth. God may be found doing some things—and showing up in some places—that will surprise you. What is powerful is watching what God does *after* acting in a way you weren't expecting. Tracking God in the full story can give you confidence in trusting His plan, even if it is different from the one *you* had.

The practice of seeing where God is in your story while you are living it is similar to observing an artist while he or she paints. After you've looked back and seen some of the artist's finished paintings, you have more hints and clues about how the artist works. When you look back at the ways you have seen and experienced God, you will know what to look for, when to wait, and when to leave room for new things to be seen. You will know you can trust the way the painting comes together—even if the process getting there is different from what you thought.

In the remaining chapters, you will not only see where God has moved in your past, but also learn perspectives and skills to use in looking for where God is moving in your life now and in the future. Each chapter will conclude with a section called "Moving Forward" that will allow you to practice a new way to watch for God.

Whether you go through this book by yourself or with a group, I wrote it so you would have proof of the ways God has been present to you. This will be a chance for you to piece together your God story, and my hope is that you will be encouraged by what you see. Maybe you'll even write a book yourself that will begin with what you discover here.

In the meantime, the practices you will learn will grow your ability to experience God more tangibly, because you will know what to look for in order to see Him. Like Jacob, you will be able to say, "Surely the Lord is in this place."

Read on and you'll see how.

two

Hearing God

If you've been in or around church for any length of time, you may have heard someone say, "God spoke to me."

Depending on how—or from whom—you heard these words, it could make you feel several things:

skeptical

curious

envious

uncomfortable

Since you are the coauthor of this book, circle the word above that best describes how you would feel if someone said this. (Feel free to add another word that isn't listed.)

Now here's another question:

Have *you* ever had the experience of God speaking to you? YES / NO

Whether your answer is yes or no, I'm going to go out on a limb and say I think you *have* heard God speaking. But hearing God's voice requires recognizing God's voice. So if you're not sure whether you've heard God, and you want to be able to recognize when it happens, I hope this chapter helps. I hope it will also reveal some of the ways you have heard God speak and just weren't aware of it.

Pete Greig, author of *How to Hear God* (one of the best books on the subject), writes,

> Learning to hear God's voice—his word and his whisper—is the single most important thing you will ever learn to do. . . . [It is not] an optional extra for wild-eyed mystics and those who happen to be spiritually inclined. Hearing God is essential to the very purpose for which you and I were made.[1]

It seems that in a book about tracking God's presence, learning to hear and recognize God's voice is a critical skill.

Hearing God speak to you is a little like being in a foreign country surrounded by people speaking a different language and suddenly hearing someone in the crowd speak your language. Other conversations may be happening, but they fade to a lower volume. When someone speaks your language, your ears tune in. It's almost as if the volume is turned up on those particular words.

But how do we recognize God's voice? Is it audible? Does it come through other people? Do you hear it in the Bible? Is it a nudge or a feeling? A stirring to do something?

Yes.

It can be all those things. God's voice rings out through nature and people, Scripture verses and dreams, preaching and prophecy. But God's voice can—and does—ring out *without* people hearing it. Because hearing comes through recognition.

Psalm 19 states, "The heavens declare the glory of God; the skies proclaim the work of his hands. Day after day they pour forth speech; night after night they reveal knowledge" (vv. 1–2).

And yet, many don't hear it.

The truth is, we wake up each day to God shouting, "Here I am!" because of our existence. We live on a planet that spins around the sun with exact precision, in a body that breathes because a thousand perfectly timed details are instigating that breath, in a world filled with mountains and oceans and new life miraculously being formed every day. Yet most of the time, we hardly blink at the wonder—if we even acknowledge it as wonder at all.

Until we recognize God's voice, it is unintelligible and relegated to the background, like the *wah wah wah* of Charlie Brown's invisible teacher in the old comic strips. We don't hear what is being said because we don't recognize the voice.

Here's your first exercise: Go outside. (Just so you know, the rest of the questions in the book will not tell you where to go, but for this exercise, you need to be outside.) If you are in a place where you can't go outside, mark this page and come back to it.

Once you are outside, if you're surrounded by buildings, go to a spot where you can look up or out and see some of nature around you—any tree or lawn will do. Now, sit for five minutes in silence and take note of every sight and sound you hear and see.

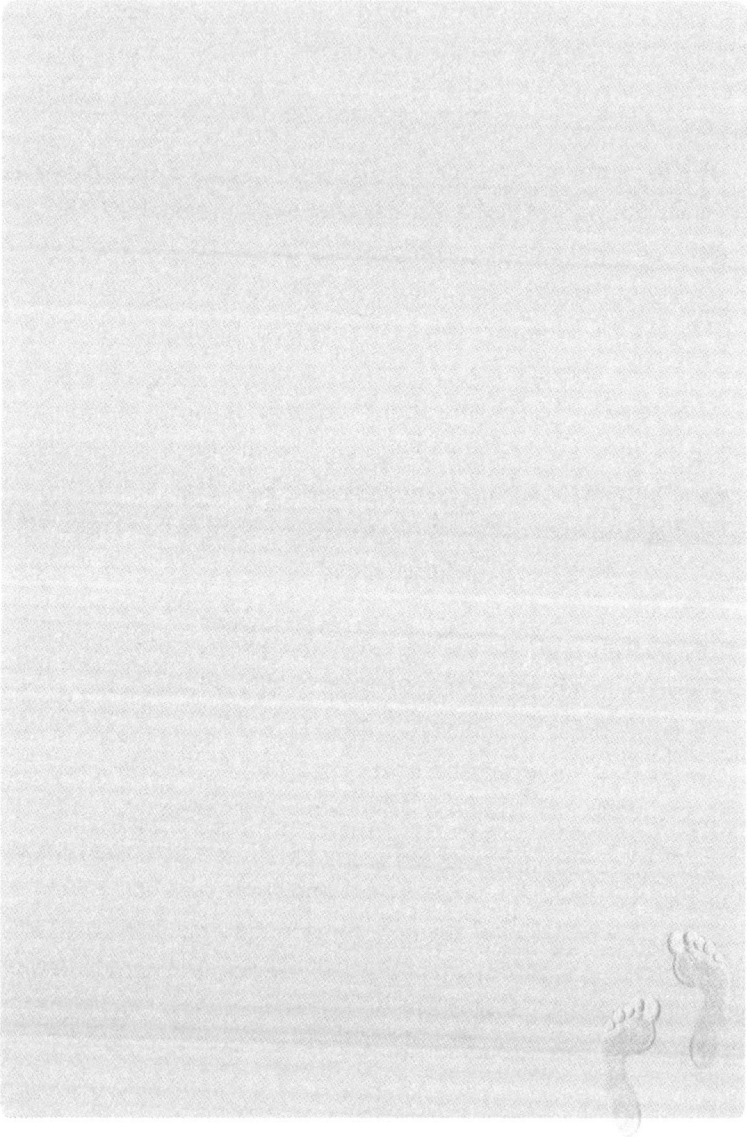

After you've made your list, answer these three questions:

1. What did you hear that you don't usually hear?

2. What did you see that you don't usually see?

3. What sight or sound did you observe that a human being didn't create?

Creation is a good place to start when you are learning to tune in to God's voice. In Romans 1:20, Paul writes,

> For since the creation of the world God's invisible qualities—his eternal power and divine nature—have been clearly seen, being understood from what has been made, so that people are without excuse.

Paul makes the case that because of creation—and all that is happening around us, every person has heard God speak. And yet you and I both know that not every person *thinks* they've heard God speak.

The experience of learning to hear God's voice is illustrated in the story of Samuel in the Old Testament. The first three times Samuel hears from God, he doesn't know it's God. Eventually, he grows up to be a prophet and becomes a professional at hearing God's voice. But at first, like many of us, he has to learn how to recognize God's voice.

If you look at Samuel's first encounter with God (1 Samuel 3), you'll learn three helpful insights that can guide you in recognizing God's voice, and in what to do when you think God might be speaking to you:

- God repeats Himself until Samuel hears Him.
- Someone else helps Samuel identify God's voice.
- God speaks more when He sees that Samuel is listening to Him.

The most important thing we see in Samuel's story is that God wants to be heard. It may comfort you to know that God wants you to hear Him as much as you want to hear God.

God calls Samuel's name repeatedly and persistently in the passage until Samuel realizes it is God speaking. When God is trying to tell us something, it's likely we will hear from Him again and again. By repeating Samuel's name until he responds (vv. 4–10), God is letting Samuel know that he is being summoned, and God has a message just for him.

This is where the second insight from the passage helps: Someone comes alongside Samuel in discerning God's voice. Three times Samuel hears his name and thinks Eli the priest is calling him, so he gets up each time and goes to Eli's room. Finally, Eli realizes what's going on and helps Samuel understand that God wants to communicate with him. We often need the same assistance when we hear from God—especially at first.

So that leads to this next question.

Do you have anyone in your life who has helped (or could help) you recognize God's voice? YES / NO

If you've ever thought you heard God say something, have you shared it with someone who helped you understand what you heard? YES / NO

Whether you have solicited help in hearing God or not, write down the name of a person (or people) you know who has some spiritual maturity and might be able to help you in discerning God's voice. It might be a mentor, or just someone you look up to spiritually. (If no one comes to mind immediately, keep thinking about this.)

After Samuel gets guidance from Eli, he hears from God again, and this time he answers. He responds with these words: "Speak, for your servant is listening" (1 Samuel 3:10). Note that when Samuel responds with receptivity, God continues with what He wants to say to him. God speaks when we are listening.

So now it's your turn to reflect on a time you felt that God might be speaking to you. Even if you aren't completely sure it was God, write down what God said.

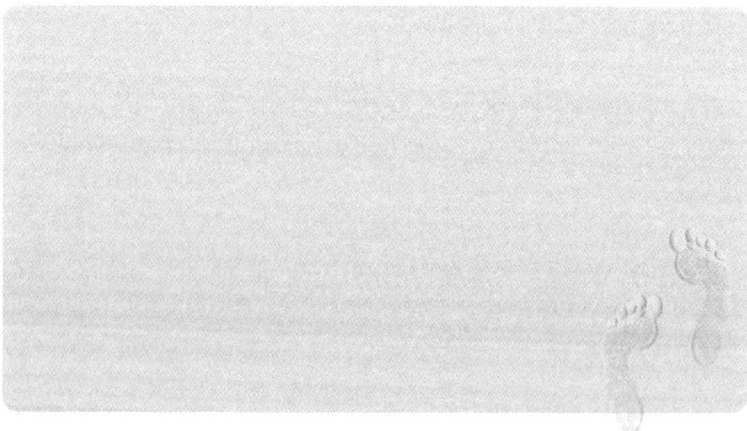

If you can't think of a time, remember: It could have happened in church or out of church; it could be something said to you by a friend or a stranger, something you heard in a sermon, or even something you heard when you were alone. Don't force it, but go back and write down anything that comes to mind.

Since it is our receptivity that makes space for God to speak, here are some more questions to reflect on:

On a scale of 1–10, how receptive are you to hearing from God?

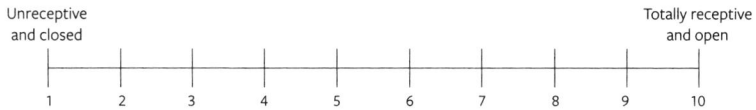

Unreceptive
and closed

Totally receptive
and open

1 2 3 4 5 6 7 8 9 10

Do you have any reservations about God speaking to you? What (if anything) blocks you from being open to it?

Presuming that hearing God requires recognition, would you say that you recognize God's voice when He is speaking to you?

Never — Hardly ever — Sometimes — Often — Always

Don't be discouraged if you don't recognize God's voice as often as you'd like. The rest of this chapter will explore some of the specific ways God speaks to us—partly to prod you more about how God may have spoken to you. Throughout the Bible, we can observe that God's voice is directional, sometimes correctional, and almost always hopeful. You may have had the experience of God bringing to your mind something you weren't thinking about before, or rousing your heart with a feeling you can't shake. But if the tone is accusing, demeaning, or degrading, it is likely not God,

We all need an Eli in our lives to help us discern God's voice. And if it seems clear that God *is* speaking to you, you may also need help identifying what God wants you to do. Because hearing God often stirs a response.

What It's Like to Hear God

I think I need to go up there and do this.

These were the words pounding in Chrissie's heart that ultimately pulled her out of her seat and led her to the foot of the stage. As she describes it, they weren't words spoken *out loud*, but words that bubbled up *inside* her heart. That day, she became the first person in our church to volunteer to run a marathon to raise money for clean water in the Democratic Republic of the Congo.

The DR Congo was introduced to our church community because the families there had to travel three miles for clean water. Worse yet, children who made that trek were at risk of being kidnapped and sex trafficked when they were sent by their parents to get water and bring it home.

When Chrissie came to church that day, she had twenty-six dollars in her bank account and two children in her care because her husband had recently left her. As the man onstage talked about mothers risking their children's lives to get what they needed to survive, the volume of his words turned up. Her own struggle was part of what pulled her to the stage.

Chrissie became the marathon team captain that year, and it turned out to be the beginning of a giant movement. In the years that followed, hundreds of people from our church ran that same marathon and raised over one million dollars toward this cause. Chrissie couldn't see all that God would use her for when she felt moved to get out of her seat and do something. She just knew God was speaking—and she responded to what she heard.

There is a phrase I learned in seminary that describes when God takes words that are spoken by others and uses them to speak to us. It's called an *agogic moment*—when the volume gets turned up and we have a recognition that **what we are hearing is for us**. The phrase was used by my professor, Ray Anderson, who got it from a book by French author Jacob Firet titled *Dynamics in Pastoring*.[2] Professor Anderson described it as the moment we suddenly feel God is addressing us, for the purpose of provoking us toward a response. It happens when something we hear connects with us in a deep and profound way. As with hearing your native language in another country, you become tuned in to what is being said because it feels like it's for you.

Have you ever had this experience of hearing something that felt like it was for you? YES / NO

If so, what did you hear?

What (if anything) did you do about it?

When we first hear what God is saying to us, we may not be ready for it. We may be afraid of what we are hearing, or need some time to respond. God is patient—and often brings His message back around if it's for us.

Just after I turned thirty, I got a call from a youth pastor about an opportunity to move to the Bay Area to take a youth ministry position. I was living in Orange County at the time, and though I had just graduated from seminary, I had never led a group on my own. After politely saying no, I hung up the phone, and suddenly I could not think about anything but this job opportunity. After a day of this weight on my heart, I sheepishly called the youth pastor and said, "I think I need to come check it out." It was a pivotal move for me—and one I almost missed with my initial response. God kept speaking to me by pressing in on my heart—and it led me to change my course and take the job.

Have you ever had an experience like that, when you felt you made the wrong decision? Or felt pulled to do something that you've resisted? If so, what happened?

Did you change your decision? YES / NO

If you missed the opportunity to change your decision, what happened next?

Our experience of hearing and responding to God, like Samuel's, is a process. After Samuel heard from God and finally recognized His voice, God continued to speak to him throughout his life. Samuel learned to listen to God—even when God was telling him something he didn't initially agree with or wouldn't have thought to do. That kind of relationship with God came from Samuel's increasing receptivity and trust. It's the same for us.

Our receptivity and trust increase as we learn to tune in to the different ways God speaks.

Hearing God Through Scripture

God doesn't just speak through what we hear, but also through what we read—and one of the clearest ways to hear His voice is through Scripture. There are times when you read something in the Bible and it's as if the words on the page become bold. You feel the words are meant for you.

My friend Jon had that experience when he felt stirrings to leave his thirteen-year position as youth pastor at his church and do something that felt like a huge risk. Because Jon was not raised in church, he had a heart for reaching unchurched people, but the thought of starting something on his own made him feel overwhelmed. Eventually the roadblocks that kept him from stepping out were slowly removed: His church raised money to support him, and a good friend offered to co-pastor and help him. A group of people were even willing to leave the church and follow him, but Jon still felt he needed some added certainty to take this step of faith.

One day as he was reading in Ecclesiastes, he came upon a verse that spoke directly to his struggle:

> Those who wait for perfect weather will never plant seeds; those who look at every cloud will never harvest crops.
>
> Ecclesiastes 11:4 NCV

There it was: Jon's hesitation clearly stated in Scripture. It was the impetus he needed to step out and plant the church.

Seven years later, Jon called me and asked if I wanted to come work at the church he had planted. I took the job, married there, and raised a child in that church, and our boy got baptized when he was seventeen years old. Today, the church has been going strong for twenty-six years, baptizing hundreds of children and adults and becoming well-known for reaching unchurched people. Jon would say it started with the impetus God gave him from a perfectly timed verse.

So now, take a minute and think back to whether there has ever been any verse or passage in Scripture that has spoken to you. It may have been directional (as it was for Jon), or correctional (convicting you about something you did or said), or hopeful (encouraging you in a specific struggle or decision).

Write down what verse or passage it was, and why it spoke to you.

God can speak by pulling on your heart, or using a verse in the Bible to speak to your personal experience. But God can also use words spoken to you by a person—about something you should do, something you want, or something you know is true. When this happens, it may take time to process or understand what God is saying.

If someone speaks into your life about the future, it is important to have a friend or mentor help you in processing it. These kinds of prophetic words need help and care in discerning them—especially when they don't unfold the way you think. Pete Greig offers some counsel about this in his book *How to Hear God*, but sharing these out-of-the-ordinary experiences with people you trust can open you up to different ways God might be speaking to you. God may have a word for you that is specific and extraordinary, even if it comes in a surprising way.

Discerning God's Voice

"The Lord is going to bring you a husband."

These words were spoken to me when I was forty years old and single, coming from a woman I had never met. She had come to a youth worker seminar I was leading in New Jersey, and I assumed she had a question about her youth ministry. Instead, she launched into a prophecy about my hidden (and greatest) longing—and completely took me off guard.

For the record, I was working at a Presbyterian church at the time and didn't have much experience with prophecy. However, I couldn't deny my hope that her words *were* prophecy because of how desperately I wanted them to be true.

She went on to say some other things I will never forget: "He will love you as Christ loves the church. He will take your head to his chest, and he will protect you. And he will be a support to your ministry."

I never got her name, but tears spilled down my cheeks after she left me. I called a good friend as soon as it happened, and she encouraged me to hold the words in my heart. If nothing else, she said, it was an encouragement that God saw me in my struggle.

Six months later, my heart was slightly pricked when I met a guy and started dating him. After he proposed and we got engaged, I was awestruck—I couldn't believe the woman's words had come true. A year and a half later, when our engagement broke up, I wanted to find the lady from New Jersey.

Um, there were a few things you left out of your prophecy.

The crazy thing is, the words she said to me eventually *did* come true. But it was only after they didn't come true. And in the five years in between, I held them as an unanswered question mark in my heart.

So let me ask you, have you ever gotten a message from God that confused you? Maybe you thought you heard something from Him, but it didn't unfold the way you thought? If so, what did you hear?

When words come from God, sometimes, like Chrissie and Jon, you'll know exactly what to do with them. But other times you'll hear something you think might be from God and you'll need to give it time. And always solicit help from people you trust.

So now take a moment and think about whether God has ever spoken directly to you through someone. This is different from hearing His voice in a crowd or reading Scripture that speaks to your heart. This is when someone has said something directly to you, and he or she says it is from God. If you've had that experience, write about it.

If you haven't had that experience, do you feel you'd be open to hearing God that way? YES / NO

Why, or why not?

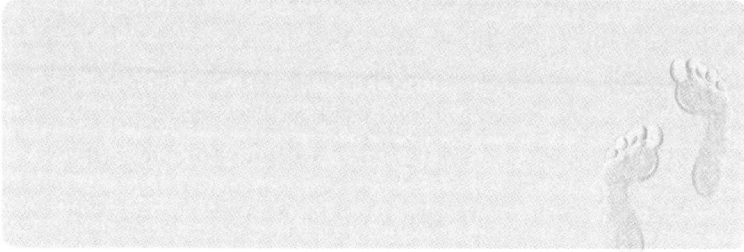

In my own experience of hearing God speak, it has mostly been a voice inside my heart rather than an audible experience. Incidents like that prophecy in New Jersey are rare. More commonly, I have the experience of having the volume turned up on a phrase I'm reading or hearing or even singing. A good practice after church, or a small group experience, is to think about what stayed with you and if it might be a word from God. Generally, the thing you remember is the thing God wanted you to hear.

Occasionally we *don't* want to hear what God is trying to say, and in that case, pay attention to the resistance you felt and why you felt it. Like anything else in our lives, God's words to us can be manipulated by our prejudices and desires, so as I've said multiple times, solicit a second opinion from someone you trust. Make sure it's someone who isn't afraid to tell you the truth, and not just what you want to hear.

When Samuel hears something that is hard to hear, particularly for Eli, it is worth noting that Eli encourages Samuel not to hide the truth from him. Eli is willing to hear whatever God spoke—even if he doesn't like what God said. Eli models for us the kind of receptivity we need in order to hear what God is saying.

Have you ever had the experience of not wanting to hear what God might have been saying to you? If so, what was it?

God may at times let you know that something you are doing is not pleasing to Him. Often that is because it's hurting *you*. Those of us who are parents know a little of what God feels when He is urging us to stop doing something that harms us. Like our own children, we might initially resist truth because growth is hard.

God patiently repeats His messages—whether His words are meant to direct you, encourage you, or correct you. With the help of someone you trust, you will be able to discern God's voice. And every time you hear and respond, you will be surprised by how much more you hear.

Moving Forward

Jesus often utters these words after He tells a story: "Those who have ears to hear, let them hear." He knows that speaking doesn't guarantee that something is heard. Communication is a two-way process, even with God, and our ability to listen is necessary for God's message to be received.

My hope is that reflecting on the ways God has spoken to you will cause you to be more open to the ways He will continue to speak to you. Since it requires a posture of listening, one step you can take moving forward is to develop a practice of listening to God. It could be anything from writing down your reflections after you've read Scripture to moving more slowly in the pace of your life. Maybe it's taking some time to sit in the morning or pausing to look around you as you transition from one event to another. Or maybe it's taking time to think for ten minutes at the end of the day how, or if, God has spoken to you.

Write down one practice you will implement to help you listen for God's voice.

God shouts through creation, moves us through His Word, and turns up the volume of people's voices to get our attention. He prods and pulls, whispers and sings, directs, corrects, and encourages, and fills us with faith and hope. God has spoken His unconditional love into the world by sending Jesus to live and die for us. It is no surprise that in John 1:1, Jesus is referred to as the Word of God.

This Word—above all words—gives our lives strength and health and courage and meaning. All we need are ears to hear Him, and the openness to listen for His voice.

three

Open and Closed Doors

God's presence is most often felt as a leading from behind, rather than as a pulling from the front. We are not puppets on a string; we are part of the equation of what happens in our lives.

We often use the phrase *open door* when something we want happens: A desired opportunity or relationship opens up to us, and we thank God for answering our prayer. A *closed door* represents the opposite: An opportunity or relationship we desire is blocked, forcing us to go a different way. Many of us believe that it's the open doors—the times we've been met with our preferred outcomes—that point to evidence of God. But have you ever thought to look for God when a door was closed?

Looking back on my own spiritual journey, it was actually a closed door that paved the way for the very best door to open. My broken engagement made room for me to consider a move and a new job, which led me to a new start and, ultimately, a new relationship. That move brought me a husband, the chance to mother a child, and many opportunities and relationships that I now can't imagine my life without.

At my wedding, I wore the dress I had bought for the ceremony planned with my first fiancé. It hung in my mother's closet (to shield me from having to look at it) for five years. So my story of marriage actually began with the closed door, a long time before the joy.

The practice of looking at the whole story, rather than a single event, helps you realize that an answer to your prayer might only have happened because something was blocked or withheld from you. God can be seen not only in what happened, but also in what *didn't* happen, when you look back.

So here is your first exercise. Look back on some of the open doors you have experienced in life—whether it was a relationship, a job, an opportunity, or something else you wanted that happened. (It doesn't have to be an exhaustive list, just the first three things that come to mind.)

1. _____

2. _____

3. _____

Now look over that list. Did any of those things happen because of something that *didn't* happen first? If so, circle it and write down next to it what door closed to make room for the open door you circled.

Tracking God in *both* the open and closed doors of your life helps you see God in opportunities and in setbacks. It also reveals that sometimes you won't see the good or bad in the story you are living now until you look back. With God, you learn to look at your life like a movie critic, who would never dare leave the theater before the end. You don't know whether something that seems bad right now might be reinterpreted as good when you look back. You won't have an accurate read on the story until you see what unfolds.

Can you think of something that happened in your life that was bad at the time, but now you realize it actually worked for your good? If so, write it down.

When you track a continuing story, you may see that some of the bad things you experienced led to some things you cannot imagine your life without. Many of the best life events happen because of what *didn't* happen first.

A verse that speaks to something bad working out for good is Romans 8:28, which says, "In all things God works for the good of those who love him." It doesn't mean all things become good, but God works *in* all things *for* good in our life. Some things that happen are hard and bad, and they can never be redefined as anything other than that. However, what happens next in our life sometimes brings a new perspective when we see what followed the hard and the bad. Staying in the story helps you see how God has used the disappointments and difficulties to work for good in your life.

Here are four things to remember about tracking God in the open and closed doors that move you through life.

1. Don't leave the story too soon.

The practice of looking back reveals how our story continued after we were prevented from something we wanted. We get a clearer perspective on what the story really was when we see what happened next. However, as I mentioned before, this doesn't mean that every sadness turns into happiness. Sometimes God is seen in what that sadness ended up bringing into your life.

One of the underrated heroes of the Bible who illustrates this is Jonathan. You may know Jonathan as David's best friend, but you may not know that he was skipped over for the throne. Jonathan was Saul's son, and he was next in line for the kingdom. However, because of Saul's reckless actions, Jonathan was the inadvertent recipient of Saul's consequences and lost his chance (see 1 Samuel 15:28). Jonathan's future as a king was a door that closed—not because of anything he did, but because of his dad's actions. And yet, as a testament to his character, Jonathan became David's closest friend and a strong supporter throughout his life.

If we stopped the story there, quite frankly it would feel a bit unfair—truthfully, it always did to me. We see enough of Jonathan's character to know he would have made a great king. It's easy to identify God's movement in David's life, but hard to see where God is for Jonathan. But further in the future of the continuing story, we can see evidence of God's work.

Jonathan has a son named Mephibosheth, who is left behind when Jonathan is killed by the Philistines. Even more tragic, Mephibosheth was disabled because he fell when his nurse was hurriedly fleeing with him. We can presume that without any intervention, Mephibosheth's life would have been tragic and marginalized. However, after Jonathan's death, David moves this sad story into something different when he asks his servants if Jonathan has any relatives left. When David finds out Jonathan has a son, he not only gives back the land of Saul to Mephibosheth, but he also invites him to eat at his table—not just once, but for the rest of his life (see 2 Samuel 9). In the continuing story of David and Mephibosheth, the kingdom privileges that eluded Jonathan were extended to Jonathan's son.

Jonathan didn't know what would happen in his future—that Mephibosheth would be orphaned when Jonathan died prematurely. But if you are (or know) a parent of a child with disabilities, you realize there is a special burden that those parents carry for how their children will be cared for after they are gone. In the story of David's inviting Mephibosheth into his home, we see God's care and attention to Jonathan, in lining up provision for Mephibosheth after Jonathan was gone.

Seeing God in the continuing story may take months or years, or possibly even a lifetime. But if you *stay in the story*, you eventually see the hand of God in what happens in time. In many of your stories, you will be able to see evidence of God's care and attention in your disappointments before your life is through.

Think back on your story. This question might take some thinking over, so feel free to pause in the book and sit in this reflection for as long as it takes. As you look back on things that have happened to you, is there a closed door that disappointed you or seemed unfair, but now, further down the line in the story, you can see something that points to evidence of God's hand? If so, what was it?

When I was engaged the first time, I was excited that I was going to be a stepmom to an eight-year-old girl. This little girl and I loved each other immediately and did many things together—and I grieved the loss of her as much as the loss of my fiancé when we broke up.

However, years later in my story, I realized that she had come into my life for a purpose that was different than I initially imagined. She made room in my heart and gave me practice for the boy God knew would one day take her place.

That's another angle on your story to think about: Have you ever faced a closed door that ended up giving you something you needed down the road? Some experience or understanding or practice for something that happened to you in the future? Something you didn't know you would need that you only see looking back?

If so, write it here.

Looking back, we always see more of what God was doing because we see what happened next in our stories. But what God did may have less to do with what happened *to* you, and more to do with what happened *in* you. This is another way to track God as the story continues in your life.

2. Look for God in what happens to you and *in* you.

Often, a closed door is accompanied by disappointment. The loss may be minimal or it may be profound. But it's fair to say you will probably live through some pain and disappointment before you're able to see God in doors that were closed.

There are times when evidence of God is not seen in what happened to us, but what happened *inside* us. A disappointment may have brought you compassion for others going through the same thing; a breakup could have helped you to find your own security apart from someone else—or a painful experience may have led you to develop in an area where you needed to grow. We sometimes find God in what He allows to happen in our lives because it pushes us toward growth.

We see evidence of this process in the story of Esau, who sells his birthright to his twin brother, Jacob, for a dish of stew because he is starving (Genesis 25:29–34). After that, he loses his blessing from his father because Jacob dresses up like him and gets there first (Genesis 27:5–29). When Jacob tricks Isaac and gets the blessing, it is terribly unfair, and we get a glimpse into Esau's rage when he decides to kill Jacob (Genesis 27:41). Because Jacob runs away and the Scriptures follow Jacob in his story, we don't hear about what happens in Esau's life for many years. When Esau resurfaces, it is when Jacob gets word that he is coming with his army of men.

Jacob is terrified to see him because he assumes Esau is as mad as he was when Jacob left.

However, when Jacob first sees Esau from a distance, Esau runs toward him and embraces him (Genesis 33:4). Through this unexpected response, we see that God has moved inside Esau's heart. So much so that Jacob proclaims, "To see your face is like seeing the face of God" (Genesis 33:10). Esau's embrace revealed that God must have softened his heart through undesired circumstances. His transformation began with the closed door of not getting his deserved blessing, and through his heartfelt reunion with Jacob, we see the evidence of a dramatic shift in Esau's life.

A loss or disappointment can be an opportunity for a new strength or character quality to be developed in you. It may be hard to see God in the closed door, but when you think about what happened *inside* you because of it, you might see evidence of God. The way you grow and change reflects God's presence in your life.

So now take a moment to think about a closed door that led to something happening inside you. It could be an area where you needed to grow, a strength you needed to develop, a compassion you did not have before, or something else. Write anything that comes to mind here.

Where or how have you seen evidence of that change in you? Has anything happened since the door closed that you handled differently because of the strength you developed? If so, write it down.

God uses closed doors to work in us, as well as to position circumstances around us. But God also uses a closed door to move us to a new chapter from a chapter we would have preferred to stay in to the end. When that door closes, in our grief and disappointment, we can't imagine what God could still do—and we might feel like life is over.

Then we wake up the next morning, and we eventually see our way to live this new chapter of life.

3. If you wake up, God's not through with your story.

The fact that your story continues after a devastating closed door doesn't take away your sorrow. God shows up in loss and pain so powerfully that I've devoted a whole chapter to it in this book. However, from another perspective, God sometimes uses loss to move us into a chapter of life we never would have experienced if a door hadn't closed.

When my father remarried after my parents' divorce, I was devastated because he married a woman who was three years older than me. The day of his wedding I was twenty-two, my father was forty-five, and his bride-to-be was twenty-five. She was also breathtakingly beautiful, while I was recovering from college weight gain and struggling to find my way in my parents' post-divorce reality. Needless to say, their wedding was one of the most painful events of my life.

However, all these years later, I look back on their wedding day with an entirely different, full-story perspective. The woman who married my dad has been a pillar in our blended family, and in my father's old age, she has stayed faithfully by his side. For me, the story of their marriage now couldn't be more different than when it began, because I could not imagine my life without her. She is not only a blessing to me because of the care she provides for my dad, but she has become one of my closest friends. I can say now that I am exceedingly grateful to have her in my life.

Often, we see evidence of God in the way time develops the story. We can see how the continued story changed Esau when he locks Jacob in an unexpected embrace. When Esau shows up in Genesis 33, it is clear he has achieved great success because he has a huge army of men with him. His attitude and achievements indicate that at some point, Esau must have let go of his anger and disappointment and allowed God work in his heart and life.

Esau's closed door of losing his birthright initially forced him into a life he neither deserved nor wanted. And yet, God used that closed door to open a new chapter for Esau—softening his heart and providing for his life. In the continuing story, we see how God worked in Esau's life.

So now take a moment and reflect on the most difficult closed door you ever experienced—something that happened that made you feel like life as you wanted it was over. Whether your closed door was a bad breakup, a divorce, an accident, an illness, or losing a job, write down the greatest loss or disappointment you have had so far that signaled to you that your life would not continue the way you wanted.

Do you see any evidence of God in what has happened since? Any new perspective that has changed the way you view the story of that closed door? If so, write it down.

The important thing to remember is that if you wake up and you're still breathing after a devastating closed door, God is still in your story. As time passes, your story may evolve and change, so don't write the ending before the story is through.

4. When you stop waking up, God's still not through with your story.

Not only does God continue to work in our story when something happens in our lives, but God's work also continues after our lifetime. Some of what will happen because of the closed and open doors we experience will only be seen after we are gone. When we track God in the things that are seen during our lifetime, we can trust that some closed doors will set up things that will be seen after our life is through. Because life here is only part of our story, some of the evidence of God's presence in our lives will only be seen after we die.

Jonathan's story reveals this truth in the continuing story of David's care for Mephibosheth. We also see God's work in the entwined stories of Rahab and Ruth, who show up way after their lifetime in the genealogy of Christ (Matthew 1:5). These continuing stories of faith reveal that your story keeps getting woven together after you are gone.

This can bring us peace when we don't see a closed door resolved—or anything good come from it—in our lifetime. Not everything is wrapped up neatly this side of heaven, but we have evidence through our past stories to trust what God will do with the ones that are not resolved. Hebrews 11 speaks of many people who died in faith, who did not see all that God ended up doing. But as Hebrews

11:4 reminds us, our story continues after death. "By faith Abel still speaks, even though he is dead," so we can trust that God will keep working in our story after we're gone. Jonathan, Rahab, Ruth, and many others reveal that truth.

For your last reflection, look back on the closed and open doors you recorded. What do you see that has happened that will impact people who will outlive you?

Can you see any story that God might be orchestrating that will be longer than your life? If so, what is it?

Tracking God in stories from your past reveals you can't judge God's movement from a single event—until you see how the story continues. As I write, we have experienced devastating fires in our state of California that burned up over fifteen thousand homes and led to unimaginable loss. But as the story continues, God will show up in people who come alongside victims, as well as in new perspectives on life and faith that will begin to surface. Endings bring new beginnings, and sometimes redefine the way we view the events of our lives.

Looking back at closed doors—and where they led you—gives you the perspective you need to suspend judgment on God's involvement until the story continues. When you see what God did that you couldn't see while it was happening, it helps you stay in the story and trust.

— — — — — — — — — **_Moving Forward_** — — — — — — — — —

Some of the doors we want to go through close, and others we never would have chosen open up to us. Life is a mixture of what we choose and what is chosen for us. Tracking God in closed and open doors shows us the importance of staying in the story to see the breadth of God's work.

When God doesn't act—or prevent, or move—the way we think God should, _at the time we expect Him to_, we often give up on Him. We might even stop thinking God is there at all. But looking back, we realize we have to wait—sometimes months, sometimes even years or decades—to see what God is up to. We can (and should) feel our disappointments and losses, but we can't let them write the final scene of God's involvement in our life. Which doors open and close is often decided for us. However, the way we respond is in our control. When a door closes, instead of trying to force it open, choose to trust. It is likely that time will bring more perspective on why the door closed.

We can decide to live in bitterness or anger over what didn't happen. But when we do that, we miss out on what God _is_ doing in our life. Past stories reveal that one door can lead to another door, and your path might even lead to a door you originally hoped would open. It's just a different timing and a different route.

Looking back also shows you that a loss or disappointment can actually turn to joy down the road because you have a new filter on your perspective. That's what makes life a journey—and you shouldn't make a final judgment on what God is doing until the end. Suspend your judgment and stay in the story with God.

Think of a story you are in the middle of living right now, where you have something you want to happen. Maybe it's a long-standing prayer, or an opportunity that you've been waiting for, or a relationship you desire. If something comes to mind, write it down.

Try an experiment of living this current story in trust—and accepting what happens even if it's different from what you wanted. Continue to track God by journaling what occurs as you move on. Whether it's something that happens in you or around you, try to notice God's involvement. See what develops as the story continues, and how (or if) things change.

There are things God sees about our story that we can't see while living it. The more we stay in the story and trust Him, the more we see what God sees.

four

Timing and "Coincidences"

The timing of events in our lives offers us a window through which to see God's presence. When something happens after it seems no longer possible or you experience a perfectly timed collision of circumstances, pausing to notice can reveal evidence of God.

God is like an invisible conductor, and when you observe an orchestration of people, events, or circumstances coming together just so, it gives you a glimpse of some kind of hidden order. We can track God in things that happen because of *when* they happen, and when you experience a surprising coincidence, you can look behind it to see the presence of God.

It's ironic that the word *coincidence*, used to secularize the unexplained, can also bring you to a place of faith—*if* you look behind the so-called coincidence to consider what it took for that to happen. Observing the timing of things happening around you can be another way to track God.

Think about the last coincidence you experienced—even if it was something small or seemingly insignificant. Maybe someone showed up at the same place at the same time as you, or you got a call or text from someone the moment you were thinking of them, or something you saw or heard connected precisely with what you were going through—anything that made you say to yourself, *What a coincidence!* Write down the first thing that comes to mind.

Think a little more deeply about it. Can you connect any dots as to why God may have caused this to happen? If so, write your thoughts below.

We are going to do more exploring in this chapter, but this is just to start you thinking about how coincidences can point to God's orchestration. God appears in ways that are only visible to you because how He appears is personal to what's happening in your life. When you look back at things that happened that seemed too perfectly timed not to be intentional, you may see evidence of God's arrangement in how things came together.

An orchestration of timing can be seen in the story of Joseph, which takes up multiple chapters in Genesis. Because so much of Joseph's life is recorded in Scripture, we are able to observe from a macro perspective how God worked. This is helpful when we can't see past the micro perspective of something hard that is happening to us, because we can be encouraged that God may be working to line things up for a convergence of timing. From Joseph's story, we learn that at any given moment, where we are may be partly because of *when* we are there.

The Right Place at the Right Time

Joseph's story begins with a dream in which he gets a message from God about his future leadership (Genesis 37). However, what happens to Joseph after this dream can only be seen as a path toward leadership when you look back. When it comes to tracking God in timing, looking back is how we get the clearest view of God's work.

After Joseph announces to his brothers his dreams of ruling over them, they throw him in a pit, then sell him to some Midianites who take him to Egypt to sell him into slavery. In Genesis 37:36, we learn that the man who buys Joseph is Pharaoh's official Potiphar, the captain of the guard.

Since Egypt was considered the center of power in that day, we can see how Joseph was brought closer to that place of power by the particulars of the quest to sell him. Peeling back from the story to the geography of what happened, we can see how Joseph was brought to the right place for what God was going to do.

So here's your first question for reflection: Have you ever had a circumstance, event, or job change that moved you to a different location? Somewhere you would not have gone if this hadn't happened? If so, write it down.

Looking back, can you see how the timing of this move brought you to that place for a reason? If so, what was it?

We only see how a change in location may have positioned us for something in our future when we look back on where we were when things happened. God grows our faith when we realize the timing of when we were brought to a place played a part in what happened next.

The Egyptian official who buys Joseph is Potiphar, and he is so impressed by Joseph that he puts him in charge of everything in his household. This delegation of responsibility reveals Joseph's growth from cocky teenager to hardworking adult, which also played a part in how he advanced. However, things take a turn when Potiphar's wife uses Joseph's advancement to try to seduce Joseph, and even though Joseph resists her, she tells her husband that he raped her. Potiphar believes her, and through Potiphar's wife's false testimony, Joseph is unfairly sent to jail. From a micro perspective, this must have made Joseph feel forgotten by God.

However, from a macro perspective, prison is exactly where Joseph needed to be to meet the people who would position him for future leadership. And that brings us to another way to observe God in the orchestration of our lives.

The Right People at the Right Time

The timing of Joseph's imprisonment eventually reveals that Joseph is in the right place to meet the right people. But we only see that by watching what happens over a period of time. When he was sentenced to prison, Joseph must have felt abandoned and alone.

God's orchestration of timing unfolds with twists and turns, and we don't necessarily see His hand in the midst of what is happening. Where we see God is in the details of how things ultimately converge in our lives. The fact that Joseph's imprisonment happens when Pharoah's attendants are in jail shows God's orchestration—even though what happened to get Joseph there was unfair to Joseph. Sometimes we have to pull back from the particulars of what happens to us in order to see God's plan in what unfolds in our lives.

Because Potiphar was Pharoah's official, Joseph was sent to the king's prison. So right from the start, in all that happened to Joseph, God's orchestration can be seen. Joseph was eventually able to meet two officials from Pharoah's palace, the cupbearer and the baker, because they were sent to prison while Joseph was there. The two men have troubling dreams during their prison stay, and with Joseph there to interpret them, it sets the stage for Joseph's rise.

Think about whether you've ever connected with someone because you were in the same place at the same time. Because of the timing of you both being there, it felt like this "coincidence" was meant to be. Maybe God was orchestrating your meeting for something that would happen because of it. If any person comes to mind, write their name down—and anything that happened when you connected.

Sometimes these kinds of coincidences are small and incidental. Other times, a convergence happens that is so significant, it points to God. Noticing your smaller coincidences will help you see the bigger convergences that bring you a faith-producing view of God.

A year after I married Jere, I was invited to speak at a college chapel at a school his stepdaughter had attended two years earlier. Jere had raised two stepchildren along with fathering a son, but Jere's stepdaughter had been estranged from him since his divorce. He was brokenhearted because for twelve years, he had been the only dad present in her life.

When I was invited to speak at this college, we both knew Jere's stepdaughter had left the school two years prior. However, in a convergence of perfect timing, she happened to be visiting a friend at the college the day I showed up. When this friend came to chapel and saw that I was speaking, she sent Jere's stepdaughter a text.

She came to chapel and waited in line to meet me, and I was so stunned when she said who she was that I grabbed her and hugged her. While we were locked in an embrace, I briefly thought I might have freaked her out with my overenthusiastic response. What actually happened was that the two of us forged a friendship that eventually brought Jere back into her life as a father. In the years since that meeting, she has become such an integral part of our family that when she had a daughter of her own, she grafted us in as grandparents, and we are thrilled to be a significant part of her child's life.

And it all started with a perfectly timed chapel talk that my husband and I suspect all along God had planned.

When you look back on some of your coincidental convergences, it offers you a window into God's orchestration. But you have to pause in order to notice these convergences; otherwise you miss what God has there for you to see.

Has any memory stirred in you of someone being in the same place at the same time as you that may have led to something significant? A chance meeting that led to a rekindling of a relationship, or even a connection with a stranger that brought someone you knew back into your life? Any unexpected meeting that you suspect might have been orchestrated by God? Write down whatever comes to mind.

Another key insight from Joseph's story is that it's not just the places we want to go that bring evidence of God's timing, but also the places we *don't* want to go. We might not have wanted to be where we were, but looking back, we can see why God had us there.

The Wrong Place at the Right Time

From one angle, it could look like Joseph was put through slavery and jail to get where God was taking him. But God didn't cause the circumstances that happened to Joseph; they happened because of envy, jealousy, and lies. Where we see God emerge is in how He exercised His sovereignty *through* those circumstances to work in Joseph's life.

God can work His good in everything that happens to us. So the places that we don't want to go are just as likely as our desired places to reveal a glimpse of God. And often the way we see God in those places is through timing.

Certainly that was true for Gary, who seemed to be destined from birth for a top rank as a Marine Corps officer. His dad had been a three-star general under Norman Schwarzkopf, and Gary had hit all the marks for following in his steps. However, after thirty years of service, Gary ended up retiring as a colonel and never received the coveted appointment to general that everyone thought was in the bag.

Soon after that, Gary applied for a job at San Diego County, but it was not the job he had worked for or wanted. He was hired as chief resilience officer, and after he started, several fires broke out during a California drought. Gary spent many hours assisting the firefighting efforts, and his leadership skills were so clearly displayed that he was pulled out of his position to help coordinate the COVID crisis. While millions of people stayed sequestered in their homes for months, many San Diego businesses were losing their leases, and Gary found a way to help them survive.

On the heels of COVID, the border crisis began escalating, and thousands of people were coming into San Diego with no plan or provision. Gary was called to facilitate the details of managing the crisis and giving these immigrants some kind of start. While most people took to social media to proclaim whether they were for or against what was happening, Gary was on the ground doing what was needed to help manage the people who were coming. From all these efforts, Gary was eventually hired to a permanent position of leadership that didn't exist before he arrived. It was the timing of events that showed Gary why he was brought to this place to exercise his leadership. However, San Diego County wasn't the place he had wanted to go or ever imagined he would be. Looking back, he sees now that it was the right time and place to help many people because of the skills he had acquired.

Take a minute and think about whether you've had to go somewhere you didn't want to go, but now see in the timing of being there that it was where you needed to be for a reason. If anything comes to mind, write it here.

What happened after you arrived that showed you it was right for you to be there?

For Joseph, it was being in slavery and in prison that led him to where he was going. For most of us, it is usually a place or set of circumstances that are not quite as severe. However, even after such bleak circumstances, Joseph was able to utter these words to his brothers:

> You intended to harm me, but God intended it for good to accomplish what is now being done, the saving of many lives.
>
> Genesis 50:20

More than likely, you also can look back on being somewhere you didn't want to go and see how you needed to be there for a specific reason. It might not have been as big as saving many lives, but if you track what happened further down the road, you may see the significance of being in this "wrong place" in the way things unfold.

The timing of events in our lives often brings the presence of God out of the shadows. We can also see God emerge after the timing of what we wanted to happen runs out. Long waits (if we stay in them) can lead us to our grandest view of God.

The Same Place for Too Long a Time

Each place that Joseph ended up brought the right people at the right time for what would happen. But Joseph had to remain in jail for too long a time to sustain any logical hope. Joseph's two-year prison stay (Genesis 41:1) gives us another insight into how God uses timing. When God shows up after it seems too late, our faith is transformed when we see why.

Before Pharaoh's cupbearer is released from the jail, Joseph reminds the cupbearer not to forget him. By the time the cupbearer finally remembers him, it's clear that for two years the cupbearer did not do what Joseph implored. It's likely that Joseph had given up, having undoubtedly realized what Genesis 40:23 confirms: "The chief cupbearer, however, did not remember Joseph; he forgot him."

But what if the cupbearer had remembered him before the two years were up?

If he had tried to help Joseph get out *before* Pharaoh had his troubling dream, Joseph may have simply been released from prison. But the timing of the cupbearer's remembering Joseph was exactly right for Joseph's skills to shine. Joseph is released to interpret Pharaoh's dream—and he's immediately elevated to become Pharaoh's right-hand man because of what the dream conveys.

Sometime during the two-year wait, Joseph had probably let go of his hope for release before God made it happen. When the timing seemed too late, the prison door was opened at Pharaoh's request. The convergence of Pharaoh's dream and the cupbearer's memory brought Joseph to the palace at just the right time for the impending famine—when Joseph's leadership was needed most.

Think back to a time when you felt you were in a holding pattern, a wait, or a struggle that felt too long, but that, in looking back now, you can see how the length of time was needed because of what happened next. Write about it here.

What happened to your faith during that time? Did you ever feel like giving up on God?

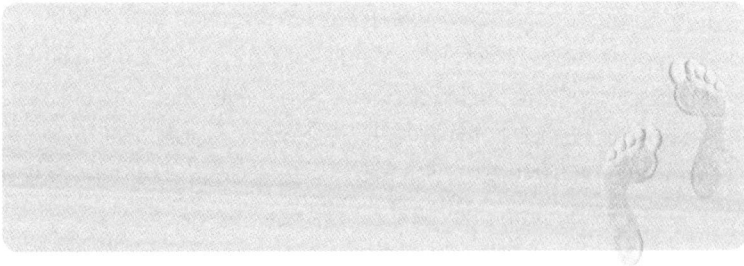

Can you see anything God did in you, around you, or through you because of this wait? If so, write about it below.

We see many other examples of what long waits produced throughout Scripture. The backdrop of disappointment and loss seems to be where God loves to surprise us most. We see it with Abraham and Sarah in the birth of Isaac. We see it in a different way with Mary and Martha, who waited through Jesus's delay only to see their dead brother, Lazarus, returned to life. And we see a third way in Anna and Simeon, who waited many long years for the Promised Child and were able to see Him just before the end of their lives. Long waits bring the treasured glimpses of God.

Walking down the aisle at forty-nine years old, I also experienced the fruit of God's waiting room. Though it was an age few girls dream to be married at, it was an age that made it apparent to everyone that no matter what we are praying for, we should never give up. Through the lens of "too late," we get our clearest view of God.

When time makes things seem impossible, God makes Himself most visible. When our timeline has run out, God has an opportunity to shine.

Moving Forward

God's orchestration of timing brings a sense of holy anticipation to our faith journey. At any moment, some unexpected meeting or coincidence might show that God is there. I just experienced this myself while I was finishing this chapter on a layover between flights.

A young man who was headed home to Ghana struck up a conversation with me, and I learned he had been through a bad breakup. We happened to sit next to each other at the airport, and when he found out I was a Christian, he shared that he was struggling with his faith. Specifically, he said he was struggling with God's timing— and when he found out that was the title of my recent book, he felt that God had brought us together. His mother had told him she was going to fast and pray for his journey—and somehow, in a crowded airport, we ended up next to each other for the thirty minutes we were there.

Needless to say, the young man's struggling faith (along with my own faith) took a small leap.

When you learn to watch for God in timing, you can trust that when things take too long, God may be orchestrating it for a purpose. Instead of forcing your own agenda and timeline, make room for what you do not yet know. Become a keen observer of what is going on around you to understand what God might want to do with you. At any given moment, God may do something unexpected that shows you He is there.

And the next time that happens, come back to this page and write it down right here.

five

Mirrors and Cliffs

There are two risks in life that position us to experience God's presence. One is to do something you are afraid to do. The other is to look at something inside yourself that you are afraid to see.

You might think it odd that I pair inward risk with outward risk in the same chapter. But they both require a vulnerability that moves us to feel our need for God. We don't *know* we need God until we feel a need for God. A risk forces us to encounter this need.

When we have to look inside ourselves at some truth, or face a challenge that pushes us beyond our capability, we are brought to a similar precipice. Whether or not we move forward will determine how much evidence of God we see. It's possible to live a complacent, safe life and never experience what God is able to do for you. Take a risk to do something uncomfortable and you make room for God.

This is probably the most personal chapter because it will involve at least some level of vulnerability. You will look back at things that you were afraid to do, as well as times when you were confronted with something you didn't want to see in yourself. My hope is that you'll discover that behind every risk you take is a God whose goal is to move you toward freedom. Each time you don't let fear stop you, the freer you become.

To get started, write down something you've been afraid of—whether it's something you haven't been able to do or something you have not wanted to address inside yourself. Write down the first thing that comes to mind.

What makes it hard for you?

Let me begin by saying that if you can't think of anything you're afraid of or need to face, buckle up and get ready to do some deeper reflection. This chapter will push you to look at what I'm pretty sure is there. And if you've already identified a fear or reluctance that you struggled with, my hope is that God will give you new revelations about how present He has been (and can be) in your fear.

Risks reveal God's presence because they take you to a place you can't go by yourself. The bigger the risk is for you, the more of God you need.

But the first step in risk taking is not God's—it's yours.

Mirrors

I was sitting in my sorority room in college when I got the call from my mom that would change the course of her life. She was quiet and calm, and said matter-of-factly that she was going to check herself in to a hospital rehab center for a month. She had informed the friend who was taking her there not to listen to her if she tried to resist going. She knew this moment of clarity might not last—and did everything she could to protect her brave choice.

"Since I will be in the hospital for four weeks, I need you to come home and take care of your little brother." I was a student at UCLA, which was only an hour away, so I gladly agreed to the task. That was forty years ago, and it was the last day my mom ever had a drink.

A few months before I got that call, I had become aware of her problem. All the adults in my family drank, so I didn't really notice her drinking when I was growing up. But she knew deep inside that her drinking was different, and eventually, I realized it too. She said in retrospect that it gave her courage she needed to live her life.

Once when I came home from college to visit, I remember leaving *The Up and Outer*, a book with a cover of a man crawling up a martini glass, strategically placed on a coffee table in front of the television. My mom was furious when she discovered my subtle intervention. But a few weeks later, she made the brave decision to admit her need for help. It was the most courageous thing I ever saw my mom do.

When I think of mirrors, I think about the day my mom called me. She took such a vulnerable and humble step, and set an example for me to look honestly at things that were hard to see in myself. Though my struggles have been different, she gave me the courage to face things that I resisted looking at by modeling it. And watching what unfolded in my mother's life showed what that courage could become. She went back to school to get her bachelor's and master's degrees, and eventually become a therapist specializing in drug and alcohol abuse in families. The year she passed away, I received notes from several people about the impact she had on their lives. Her life showed me what God is capable of doing in and through us when we face the truth about ourselves.

Richard Rohr, in *Breathing Under Water*, writes, "'The truth will set you free' as Jesus says . . . but first it tends to make you miserable."[1] Often it's the miserable part that keeps us from facing the truth. But just past the miserable is a freedom that only the miserable makes possible. Facing the truth may make you feel naked and vulnerable, yet that very place is where you experience the deepest encounter with God.

So here's your first reflection: Have you ever had someone con-
front you with something hard to see in yourself? YES / NO

(Note: It doesn't have to be an addiction; it could be something
you do that is off-putting to others but you don't realize it.)

If yes, how did you respond?

When it comes to hearing the truth about yourself, do you generally feel that you are open and self-aware, or closed and defensive?
Make a mark below where you would put yourself on this scale:

Closed/
Defensive

Open/
Self-aware

(If you want to take a step further, ask someone close to you to
mark where they see you. Sometimes we think things about ourselves that are different from what others see.)

We are going to move into some specific ways that God leads us
to a mirror. With the help of two short stories, you'll consider whether

God has used either of these ways to work on you. Whether you've experienced someone telling you the truth, or a person showed you the truth, I'm hoping you'll see God behind what happened. The refining that transpires from looking honestly in a mirror helps us become the best and truest version of ourselves.

Hearing the Truth

When David is first confronted about his adultery with Bathsheba, his reaction illustrates how much we can be blinded by our own denial. Nathan tells David a story about a rich man stealing a poor man's precious lamb that obviously mirrors what David did, but David doesn't recognize himself in the story at all (2 Samuel 12). He responds by burning with rage toward the man who represents him, telling Nathan he should be killed as punishment. When Nathan says, "You are the man!" David is directly confronted with the truth about himself.

David's immediate response is profound remorse—exposing his tender heart and revealing how seeing the truth about ourselves can make us miserable. But in the chapters that follow, we see that truth eventually sets David free. It may be the clearest place in Scripture where we witness a mirror bringing someone to freedom after being faced with the truth.

If you are not familiar with that story, you can read the details in 2 Samuel 11 and 12. In contrast to all the great things David did, this was not his finest hour. However, these chapters serve as a poignant example of how seeing the truth not only moves us toward confession, but also freedom.

So now it's your turn to get honest about your self-awareness. Think back to a time when someone confronted you with something you did or said, or a behavior that negatively impacted people around you. Even if you didn't fully agree with it, answer the following questions.

Who confronted you—and what did the person say?

How did you respond?

Whether you responded positively or negatively to what was said to you, did God use it to prod you toward seeing something about yourself? YES / NO

If so, what?

Mirrors are not often handled graciously at the beginning. It's natural to feel defensive; what matters is what you do next. If you never stop and consider whether there is some truth to what's being said to you, you may not be open to seeing yourself honestly. It takes courage and humility to look at things we don't want to see.

Years after my mother's recovery, she and I were on a walk one day, and she gently told me that she had observed some control issues in my behavior. She was concerned that they might be spilling into my relationships or other areas of my life. I'd love to say I received her words graciously, but I can still remember the anger and indignation I felt when she said it. Only later did I have the courage to realize she was right.

Be gentle with yourself if hearing the truth has made you angry. It might be worth exploring what's been said to you—especially if you've heard it more than once. Asking someone you trust who will tell you what you need to hear, and not just what you want to hear, will allow God to lead you past your defensiveness. What initially may be uncomfortable for you to receive can ultimately set you free to grow and change.

Seeing the Truth

Another kind of mirror God uses is indirect—it's when you cross paths with someone who has characteristics similar to yours. We see this in the story of Jacob after he has run away from his family and ends up working at his uncle Laban's house.

Laban deceives Jacob with Leah the same way Jacob did when he dressed up as Esau to trick his father into giving him Esau's blessing (Genesis 27). After Laban's agreement with Jacob to marry Rachel, Laban replaces Rachel with Leah and tricks Jacob into marrying her instead. (You may need to read that twice). When Jacob sees he has married Leah and not Rachel, he is outraged, but it gives him an opportunity to feel remorse for what he had done to Esau. Jacob was finally experiencing what it was like being on the other side of deceit. God provided an indirect mirror to Jacob by bringing someone with similar deceptive qualities into his life (Genesis 29:25).

Because we tend to be most repelled by people who mirror our worst characteristics, Jacob has great disdain for Laban. Knowing what Jacob did prior to working for Laban, it seems his disdain is because of what he doesn't want to see in himself.

As you look back, can you think of anyone God may have put in your life to show you something about yourself? It might not be as bad as deception, but it could be some other behavior that is negatively impacting your relationships. If so, write below who it was. (If you can't think of anyone, consider someone who had a characteristic that bothered you).

As you reflect on the previous question, what purpose do you think God might have had in bringing this person into your life? Do you think it's easier for you to see something in others than it is to see it in yourself?

Can you see the good in God bringing you to self-awareness? Do you think it is better to know something you are doing that is impacting others or not to know? Why?

When Jacob finally leaves Laban's house, he still struggles with being deceitful. (You can read about his payback deception with Laban in Genesis 31.) But from that chapter forward, Jacob seems to become a softer, humbler version of himself. God used the mirror of Laban to begin peeling away Jacob's manipulative behavior. And after he experiences undeserved grace from Esau, Jacob moves forward as a father and grandfather with less manipulation and more trust.

God uses mirrors to invite us to look inward and see what needs to be changed to experience freedom. Facing the truth about our weaknesses positions us to grow. Whether it's something God wants to develop in us or eliminate, God uses mirrors not to condemn us but to mature us. If we can persevere through our vulnerability, we'll experience the gift mirrors can be.

Cliffs

When we shift from looking inward to taking a step of faith, we have an opportunity to viscerally experience what faith means. Stepping out evokes a different fear than facing the truth, but both of these actions take us to a vulnerable place. It's in that vulnerable place that we meet God.

When we stand on the edge of something we feel unequipped for, we have to overcome the fear of inadequacy in order to experience God carrying us. When we look back on something we couldn't have done alone, we see the presence of God.

The cliff of inadequacy

God moves us to the edge of what He knows we have in us. An opportunity to step out in faith calls things out of us we didn't know were there. Years ago, I was invited to become part of an all-male youth ministry speaking team because they were trying to diversify. During our first "test seminar," we passed out cards for feedback on our presentation, and then at a subsequent meeting, it was the team's practice to pass those notes around the room. One of the cards said, *"No offense to Laurie, but what is she doing on the team?"*

While the note traveled around the table with all the other cards, I did everything I could not to succumb to the tears welling inside me. At the break, I found a quiet corner in the hotel lobby (behind a tall plant) to cry. The leader of the team found me there and told me that review did not at all reflect what they felt about me. They saw potential in me, and he didn't want me to give up. Looking back, I see that was the beginning of a ten-year experience on the Youth Specialties speaking team that opened up ministry opportunities that changed my life.

Saying yes to something we know we can't do on our own provokes our trust; what God does with our yes increases our faith.

In a similar (okay, kinda different) story in Judges 6, God calls Gideon a "mighty warrior" before he has taken a single step to fight a battle. In fact, when God first addresses him, Gideon is hiding with his wheat in a winepress, which is hardly the stance a warrior would take.

The angel of the Lord who appears to Gideon knows Gideon has it in him to be a mighty warrior, not because of his skills or experience, but *because God is with him*. However, Gideon will have to grow in faith to act on what God has said. Gideon points to his disheartening circumstances and dismal qualifications to argue against what God believes about him. God persists, and after Gideon puts God through a battery of tests to get the assurance he needs, he finally answers the call.

But Gideon won't get all that he needs *until* he answers the call. That's what cliffs show us—we have to jump off before we see God move. Only when Gideon says yes to leading the army will he see what God is able to do.

What is interesting is that once Gideon concedes to becoming a leader, God peels back more of his securities (Judges 7). Gideon's army is reduced in size, and he is given less and less to rely on in order to win. When we determine to face our cliffs, God may increase the risk as much as we can stand, to show us how much He can do.

So here's your question: Has there ever been an opportunity you were given that was so over your head or beyond your skill that you knew you couldn't do it unless God showed up? If so, what was it?

If you stepped out and did it—or if you didn't do it—what happened? What (if anything) did you learn about God?

Cliffs give us an opportunity to see what God is able to do for us. The space between what you have and what God needs to do is where God grows your faith. Gideon spent a whole chapter testing God's assurance before he was willing to say yes to becoming God's warrior. But when he experienced the victory God had promised, he saw what only taking risks allows us to see.

Has God ever continued to prod you toward taking a step of faith that you've been unwilling to take?

YES — NO — NOT SURE

Here's another way to look at it: Has God ever brought an opportunity back into your life that you previously resisted—or a similar opportunity that required the same step of faith? If so, what was it?

Looking back, do you see God's involvement in continuing to prod you? If so, how?

Often, God gives us more chances to do what He wants us to do—just as God gives us multiple opportunities to see what He wants us to see. When we are blocked by our own fear or resistance, God will continue to nudge us, beckon us, and even push us through our resistance to grow our faith.

Freedom, not comfort, is God's goal for our spiritual journey. Only when we face our fear, rather than retreat from it, can we be free of fear's grip. And sometimes, we must go back to something we left behind in order to be free.

The cliff of fear

Hagar is the maidservant I mentioned in chapter 1 who calls God "the One who sees me." Her story in Genesis 16 reveals what it's like to meet God in a desperate moment and then immediately experience God calling you to do something scary to show you more of His power. Hagar had run away because she was being mistreated, and God sent an angel to comfort her in the desert. But after the angel gives her assurance that she and her son would have a future, the angel gives her a directive that must have made Hagar wince.

"Go back to your mistress and submit to her," (v. 9).

Hagar has to go back and face what she has run away from in order to freely move forward. Later, Hagar will be told it's time to leave Abraham and Sarah and make a new home. But right now, the God who has assured Hagar of His presence is telling her she must go back and face her fear.

Why would God do that?

If you stop to think about it, the only way to overcome fear is to face it. When you sidestep or resist a fear, it continues to grow. The temporary relief you may feel at the time you avoid it is replaced with discomfort when you face it again and realize your fear has grown with time. God tells Hagar to go back and face her fear so she can overcome it. She knows from her experience in the desert that God will be with her—but she needs to take the first step to say yes.

And I wonder, has God ever done that with you?

Have you ever felt that you were being nudged to face something you were afraid of? If so, what was it?

What did you do?

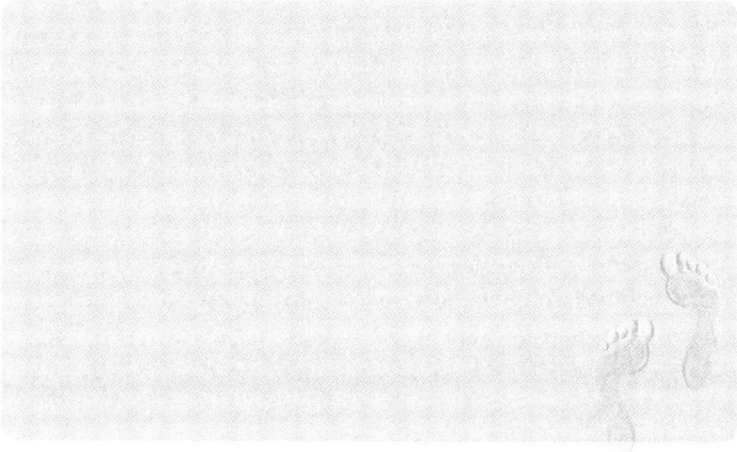

Maybe you couldn't do it, and your fear remains unconquered. Or you faced your fear, and it is no longer the stronghold it once was. Your fear may not have completely disappeared, but it does grow smaller when you stop giving it room to grow. Fear shrinks with every step of faith.

When I eventually got on that all-male (now partly female) speaking team, I started getting invitations to speak at camps and conferences. The fear I had overcome in trying out for the team began to revisit me in other forms. The first time I was asked to speak at a camp, I was too afraid to do it, so I said I had a scheduling conflict. The truth was, I made up the scheduling conflict, but God used those invitations to help me continue to face my fear. When I finally started saying yes, I just took my fear with me when I went.

With every no we utter, it becomes less likely that we will say yes to things we are afraid of. When we say yes *even if we are afraid*, we become more emboldened to face our fears. We may want to pray for God to take our fear away, but it's in the act of doing what we are afraid of that fear loses its power.

I'm sure Hagar was not without fear when she went back to live with Sarah. But you can see in the text that her fear of Sarah no longer had power over her because she never ran away again. The next time she leaves, she is sent away, and God gives her and her son the provisions they need so they can move on (Genesis 21:18–21).

Going back can sometimes be God's direction for moving forward. When it comes to conquering our fears, that may be the direction we have to go. When something continues to have a hold on us, it can keep us from things that are ahead for us. Facing our unconquered fear is what allows us to be free to move ahead.

Is there a fear from your past that you need to revisit? A conversation you need to have? A relationship you ran away from? Something you should have done but never did because you were afraid? If you have the courage, write it here. (You can put it in code so only you know what it is.)

What would it take for you to go back?

— — — — — — — — — **_Moving Forward_** — — — — — — — — —

Every time you face a cliff, your courage grows stronger to face the next one. The more you learn to move through your fear, even if you have to take it with you, the more God builds your faith. You may pray that God takes that fear away, but God often answers that prayer by having us face it. It's in the act of facing our fear that the fear subsides.

Is there something in your life right now you are avoiding or resisting that God might be nudging you toward? If so, what is it?

Whether you have identified a current challenge or encounter something in the future, try moving forward instead of backward. Lean into the challenge, even if you're not completely sure how it will work out. The more experience you have being in a position where you need to trust God, the more you will learn to trust Him. Trust grows by trust*ing*.

When it comes to facing the truth about yourself, you will find it gets easier as you increase your capacity to be vulnerable. So practice vulnerability by taking in uncomfortable truth instead of repelling it, and see how considering that truth can open your eyes. Like a new pair of glasses, self-awareness not only clarifies the view you have of yourself but also brings clarity to your relationships. It is a gift you give to your family, friendships, and workplace, because being aware of what others see brings freedom and health.

When you face your fears and insecurities instead of running from them, God will grow your courage. Fear will continue to rear its head, but each time you step out in faith, it loses a little more of its grip. With every risk you take toward vulnerability, you'll have more awareness of God's presence. There is nothing like a mirror or cliff to offer us a visceral experience of God.

six

Power in Weakness

C. S. Lewis famously wrote about God whispering in our pleasure and shouting to us in our pain.[1] But I wonder if you've also noticed that God shouts *through* our pain? A spotlight shines on our faith when we go through pain and difficulty. People lean in to see how real God is for us when other things are stripped away. In difficult times, you not only have a greater opportunity to share your faith, you also have a greater opportunity to live your faith, because pain pares things down to bring us face-to-face with the strength of our belief.

In pain, we discover things about God that we can't experience in ease and comfort. The fact that God allows us to go through pain might alienate us, but pain gives us the greatest opportunity to experience His power. Our weakness makes room for the evidence of God to be openly displayed.

Paul discovered this truth when he had a "thorn" in his flesh, which God used to teach him to embrace his weakness. In 2 Corinthians 12, Paul records the conversation he had with God that led him to change his thoughts about pain. Through his reflections, you'll have a filter to look at your own pain and see how God may have used it to reveal His presence in your life.

The Thorn Not Taken

Paul doesn't get specific about the thorn he experienced, but we know it was given to him after he experienced "surpassingly great revelations" (v. 7). He thought the reason for it was that God wanted to keep him from becoming conceited, and perhaps remind Paul where the source of his security should be found. Nevertheless, this thorn came as an interruption to the wonder and awe Paul was experiencing from what he was allowed to see.

Before we look at what happened with Paul, can you think of a time when pain or hardship interrupted you in a happy season? Maybe you were in a great relationship, successful in your career, in a good place with friends, or financially secure when something painful or humbling disrupted your life.

What happened?

Looking back, do you remember being distant from or close to God before this happened?

Did your relationship with God change after the pain or hardship? If so, how?

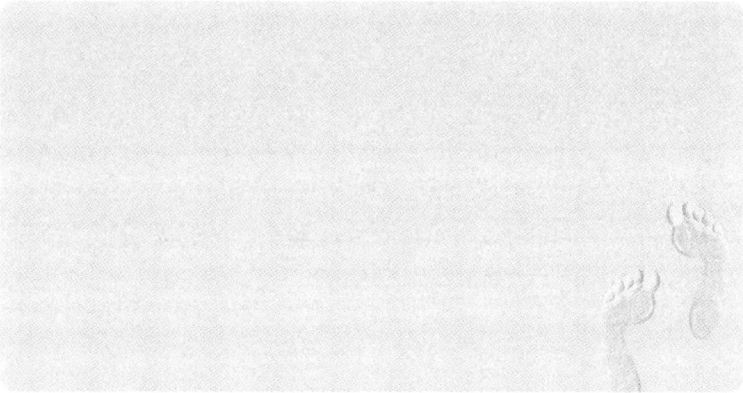

It's puzzling to think that God can use pain to draw us closer to Him, when at the beginning we feel the exact opposite. Pain feels like punishment, but it often has the effect of growing our faith. When pain interrupts us, it pushes us toward our need for God's assistance. When the things we rely on are stripped away, the void allows us to experience the sufficiency of God.

Though Satan is the source of Paul's pain, Paul goes to God to beg Him three times to remove it. God declines his request, but through this no, Paul discovers that God has a purpose for his pain. Paul might not have gotten the answer he wanted, but the answer he received changed his faith:

"My grace is sufficient for you, for my power is made perfect in weakness" (v. 9).

There are two key insights about the way God reveals Himself in this statement. Before you move on, take a minute to write them down.

1. _____

2. _____

Sometimes I find it good to rewrite a Scripture verse, particularly when it carries an unusually powerful promise. In this case, there are actually two promises about how God shows up in our time of need. We can only experience God's sufficiency when what we have is insufficient. God's power in weakness can only be displayed when we are weak. Writing a verse down ourselves imprints the truths of a verse more emphatically in our hearts. Now you'll have a chance to explore how these truths are lived out.

The Surprise of Pain

When pain strikes, it not only hurts, but it can also be terribly disruptive. There is something about going along just so that, when pain comes, it feels like an intruder stealing what we thought was ours. There is nothing like pain to break the illusion that we are in charge of our health and circumstances. It reminds us that what we thought was a given is actually a gift.

Job experiences this truth when his life falls apart, and everything he has is taken from him. Because of a conversation he knows nothing about, everything changes (Job 1), and Job never finds out why. What seems particularly unfair is that it's precisely because Job was so faithful that everything was taken away.

God doesn't cause Job's trial, but it is clear from His dialogue with Satan that God allows Job's trial. God believes Job's faith will withstand Satan's test. Although Job never abandons God, he is left with some big questions about his faith. His questions fill thirty-seven chapters, but they all carry a single theme: why?

And I wonder, have you ever asked that question of God?

Think back to a time when something bad happened that caused you to question why God was allowing it. Write it down here.

Have you ever felt angry with God—or even questioned your belief in Him because of your pain? YES / NO

If so, what happened after that? Did pain weaken your faith?

God eventually brings healing to Job—not by giving him answers or taking away all his wounds, but by giving him a different perspective. God never tells Job why he suffered; instead, God takes Job on a world tour (see Job 38–41). When Job sees his life in the context of the wider world, he realizes there is so much going on around him that he didn't know was happening, and that there might be a purpose for what he went through that he could not see.

Job responds to God with these words: "Surely I spoke of things I did not understand, things too wonderful for me to know" (Job 42:3).

Job is awestruck at what God has shown him. Even in the midst of his pain, he is captivated by everything he sees. Job uses the phrase "too wonderful," which comes as a bit of a surprise, given Job's condition.

This "too wonderful" phrase is repeated in another place in Scripture, Psalm 131. A mentor of mine alerted me to this little psalm during an especially difficult time. I had gone through yet another breakup with someone I thought I might marry, and I could not understand why God was allowing so much pain in this particular area of my life. My mentor gently reminded me that I don't see all that God sees, and took me to this three-verse psalm that David wrote:

> My heart is not proud, Lord,
>   my eyes are not haughty;
> I do not concern myself with great matters
>   or things too wonderful for me.
> But I have calmed and quieted myself,
>   I am like a weaned child with its mother;
>   like a weaned child I am content.
>
> Israel, put your hope in the Lord
>   both now and forevermore.
>
> Psalm 131

Not only does David repeat Job's sentiments of things being "too wonderful" for him to understand, but he adds something else that can be very helpful in thinking about our pain and where God is in it. He compares himself to a "weaned child with its mother"—an image that conjures up maturity. God may withhold something we want for the sake of growing us and making room for something in the future. We don't see all that will become of our pain, or how our pain might be used, and that is possibly part of the "too wonderful" that David and Job both talk about.

Can you look back on a pain that God used to do something in you or for someone else? YES / NO

If so, what was the pain God used?

Thinking about the pain of my breakup and my singleness from the perspective of what God might do with it gave me a different way to look at it. Perhaps God could see something in my pain that I couldn't see—and one day I would view my pain differently.

Weaning is done for the sake of growth; it may begin with breast-feeding, but it continues all the way through raising children. Parenting is a long series of nos for the sake of the yeses you want for your child. At the time, your children may not see the good in what you are doing because children don't have the perspective we do as adults. Being a good parent might even involve the risk of temporarily alienating your child for the sake of their growth.

Knowing God sees more than we can see allows us to respond like David to the painful things that happen to us. We can calm ourselves with the knowledge that God loves us, even if it doesn't feel like it right then. Like a weaned child, our soul learns to trust instead of demanding satisfaction. We are able to quiet ourselves with the knowledge that God is allowing this no for a reason, even if we can't see what it is.

The allowance of pain weans us from our dependence on the "Santa Claus" God, who gives us what we want when we want it. That is often our first impression of God, and when He doesn't deliver, some of us abandon our faith. We are weaned when we learn to accept something we *don't* want as having a purpose. If our suffering is not taken away, we can trust that God wants to use this pain somehow in our life.

Have you ever considered that the allowance of your pain might have a purpose in maturing your faith? YES / NO

Did (or does) that change any of your thoughts about where God is in your pain? YES / NO

Looking back, can you see how God may have been growing your faith in your painful or difficult circumstances? Is there a specific painful circumstance where you've seen this happen? If so, write it down here.

Job not only realizes God is doing more than he can see, but he ends up repenting for his limited perspective. In Job 42:3, his response changes from crying out and complaining to God to humbly trusting what he cannot see. What is interesting to note is that Job is restored and healed in the very last chapter, but it's the thirty-seven chapters of Job's painful cries that make up the bulk of his book. It's Job's struggle that is highlighted in these chapters, and for that reason his story speaks to people in pain.

Thinking back on your own life, which experiences have been used more to encourage others—your difficulties or your successes? Reflect on this below.

If you have not yet used your pain to help others, I hope the reflections in this chapter will stir something in you. Your pain finds its purpose when you take the risk to let it be used. When you allow your weakness to be showcased, you will discover something new about God.

Perfectly Shaped Pain

As God matures our faith, we may be withheld from something we want in order to offer something to others. Our struggle is perfectly designed to minister to the struggle of someone else. Recovery groups are built on this premise—that your experience will help someone in the same struggle. The burden you carry finds its purpose when you extend yourself to others who carry that burden too.

While I served on staff at Oceanhills Covenant Church in Santa Barbara, I led several mission trips, and two of those trips were to Nicaragua. However, it was the Nicaragua trip I didn't go on that was the most special because it had a specific thrust. A group of guys went with the sole purpose of bringing their friend Chris, who lived with a disability, to meet a particular need.

Teams from previous trips to Nicaragua knew about the school there called Los Pipitos because it was one of the ministry sites we visited. It was a place dedicated to mentally and physically disabled children, and the challenges that faced them in a third-world country gripped many of our hearts. So a group of guys came up with an idea: We had a resource in our church who could bring more than sympathy and money. If they could get Chris to Nicaragua, he could bring a life experience that could inspire their hope.

Even though Chris was born with cerebral palsy, his faith had inspired many people because he lived a life much more defined by his abilities than his disability. He worked a job, drove a van, and even spun vinyl at parties as the "DJ of Ability," but one thing Chris couldn't do was travel alone. An international trip would mean leaving the well-planned structure of his home, job, and transportation in Santa Barbara. So this group of guys made it their mission to get Chris to Nicaragua so he could share his inspiring testimony at Los Pipitos school.

When the students at Los Pipitos saw that Chris had boarded a plane to come all that way to encourage them, they felt seen in their struggle. Chris could communicate to them in a way no one else could because he embodied their pain. The rest of the guys on the trip made it their mission to focus on Chris—transporting him on dirt roads in a wheelchair as well as helping him dress, eat, travel, and shower. It wasn't a mission trip where the group all did ministry together; these guys went to Nicaragua to serve Chris. Helping Chris become the ambassador to Los Pipitos was the reason for the trip.

That will always be a perfect picture for me of the way God's power shines through weakness. Our particular pain is perfectly suited to help someone else. Your thorn, your struggle, your weakness is your ministry. Those who share that struggle need the wisdom, encouragement, and companionship that only you can provide.

Think more about the particular struggles you've had or losses you've been through. Write down one to three struggles or losses you've had to bear in your life. (It's okay to repeat something you've already written down in this chapter.)

1. _____

2. _____

3. _____

Have any of those struggles ever connected you with a particular person who shares a similar struggle? Circle any that have.

When we are brave enough to let our pain be used, we have a chance to see God's power at work within us and through us. And when we see what God does through our pain in other people's lives, it can highlight His presence where we never imagined He would be. What pain produces reveals the longer story and purpose of our pain.

Perfectly Shaped Comfort

Our pain shapes us so we become uniquely equipped to comfort others. Second Corinthians 1:4 says that God comforts us in all our troubles *so that* we can comfort those in any trouble with the comfort we have received from God. I saw this lived out between two young couples whose lives converged because of a shared struggle. Perhaps you'll be inspired by their story to think of a struggle that has changed you, and consider how God might want to use you.

Shannon and Dave fell in love and married in their twenties, and spent more years than they wanted watching everyone around them have children. More than once, I would catch Shannon sitting in church wiping away tears. She and Dave had wanted desperately to be parents, and the doctor could find no reason why it wasn't happening. They were told to keep trying, but endless negative pregnancy tests chipped away at their hope.

One Sunday, a woman from Angels Foster Care came to church to share a need for families who were willing to foster children for parents who couldn't care for them. Suddenly, Shannon and Dave's void seemed perfectly timed, so they felt a pull to sign up. They eventually fostered a young girl named Ruby, but because Ruby's mom couldn't take her back, they were given the chance to became Ruby's permanent family. Watching Shannon and Dave's exuberance over their daughter was blessing enough, but the unforeseen blessing was how God used them to reach another couple who were struggling in a similar way.

During a couples' dinner, Shannon and Dave were talking about Ruby, and unbeknownst to them, another couple in the midst of an infertility struggle was present at the table. Jen and Adam were still in the throes of trying for a biological child, but the memory of Shannon and Dave's exuberance took root in their hearts. Months later, when they were still childless, they signed up to foster a child, and before they had finished their paperwork, they were called about a premature baby named Caylee. She weighed only two and a half pounds at birth but had defied expectations and was ready to leave the hospital—but she had no home. Jen and Adam had plans to be away all summer, but they cancelled everything to accommodate this new baby. Eventually, they were able to adopt Caylee, and when her biological sister was available for adoption a year later, the two girls became the God-given family to fill Jen and Adam's empty home.

Not only were Jen's and Adam's lives changed by Shannon and Dave sharing their struggle, a total of five Angels Foster Care children found homes between these two couples. Shannon and Dave ended up adopting two more boys to round out their family with Ruby, and as I've watched all five kids grow up, I've seen evidence of what God is able to do with our pain. Shannon and Dave's redemptive comfort was used in a profound way—the wound they shared and the blessing they received poured through them at that dinner. And through what transpired between these two couples, God changed five children's lives.

Now it's your turn to reflect after reading this story. Has God ever refined or reshaped a desire you had by answering it in another way or at a different time? If so, describe the experience.

Can you think of someone in your life who could be encouraged by how God met you in your desire? Write their name(s) here.

God meets us in our pain and then uses that pain to bring comfort and hope to others. Perhaps that is the reason God allows thorns; they can open up a specific ministry in our lives. Paul learned that instead of begging God to take away his thorn, he had reason to delight in persecutions, difficulties, and hardship. Our sufferings open space where God can use them to shine.

If you are waiting for your suffering to be resolved before God can use it, this last story might encourage you that there is power in the middle of your story. We don't have to have all the answers about our pain for God to still use it to change someone's life.

Unresolved Pain

"It's always darkest just before the dawn" is a saying that's been used since the 1600s to help people hold on in the darkness. When things go from dark to black, this quote doesn't help as much. It can be hard to imagine that God has any purpose for what is happening when things seem to get worse—especially when we're in the middle of whatever we are going through.

That's where the book of Ruth opens up; the darkness has settled and increased for Ruth's mother-in-law, Naomi. After becoming a widow, Naomi then loses both of her sons. We get a sense of the darkness Naomi is experiencing when she tells her daughters-in-law that the Lord's hand has gone out against her (Ruth 1:13). But Ruth still saw enough of Naomi's faith to want to follow her to Israel, embrace the God she believed in, and build a new life.

I love this story because it reveals that God doesn't need our faith to be perfect in order to use us. Naomi shows us that God can use us right where we are—even if where we are isn't great. In our honest struggle with God, others see a real relationship. In the middle of your pain, your testimony of not abandoning God may be the strongest way to show your faith.

Reflect on a struggle that has continued for a while (and might still be happening). Have you ever considered that God could use you in the midst of your struggle? Or did you think you needed to wait until the struggle was resolved?

Has God ever used someone else's ongoing struggle to encourage your faith? If so, how?

God used Naomi's struggle to draw Ruth in to accompany her. Even in the midst of Naomi's doubts, God used her to bring Ruth to faith. We see this when Ruth pledges to go with her and says, "Your people will be my people and your God my God" (Ruth 1:16).

Have you ever thought you weren't responding well enough to your pain to be used by God in your struggle? YES / NO

In what ways does Naomi's story speak to any reservations you've had about how God could use you?

Ultimately, Naomi's life is changed by Ruth as much as Ruth's life is changed by Naomi. Because Naomi was vulnerable in her struggle, Ruth was able to offer her help. Naomi didn't stay alienated in her pain; she went with Ruth to Israel to get help from her community. Ultimately, Ruth marries a new husband from Naomi's community, and God uses this marriage to bring Naomi new joy.

What's beautiful about the story of Naomi and Ruth is that you see God's blessing on both of them in bringing them together. Ruth's marriage brought a new baby, which brought Naomi a second chapter of life. What neither woman could see was how their story of shared pain was woven into the bigger story of Jesus's coming. Because Naomi's community was in Bethlehem, God used Naomi's struggle in positioning Ruth to be part of Jesus's line (Matthew 1:5)

Has God ever brought you to a new community through your pain or struggle? YES / NO

Have you ever seen God use a struggle to bring you together with someone to experience new joy? If so, write about it here.

In Matthew 1:5 we get a picture of the macro story being woven by the micro story. We also see how our pain could be the starting point of a story that gives a new purpose for our life. The first chapter of Ruth seems more like an ending than a beginning, yet it was out of the ashes that a new (and ultimately bigger) story began to develop. When we risk sharing our pain, we may not be able to imagine what God has in store.

Moving Forward

After looking back on how God has used some of your thorns, perhaps you (like Paul) will look at pain differently moving forward. Paul ends his reflections in 2 Corinthians 12:10 with these words: "When I am weak, then I am strong." While we may never get to Paul's level of embracing our pain, we can at least know that if God has allowed it, there *will* be some purpose for it. Whether you experience a diagnosis, the loss of a job, or a death of someone you love, God can use whatever you go through to help someone else.

Having heard from the Lord, "My power is made perfect in weakness," Paul declares in 2 Corinthians 12:9 that from now on he will boast about his weaknesses. If you were to do the same thing, write down a pain or weakness God has used that would be part of your boast.

End this chapter by writing below any unresolved disappointment, pain, or hardship you may be currently experiencing.

If you experience God using you in the midst of your pain or hardship, come back to this page and write down what happened above Paul's words below.

When I am weak, then I am strong.

seven

When Your Script Gets Flipped

"Ladies and gentlemen, we will soon be landing in Phoenix."

I would have barely registered this announcement if I hadn't been holding a boarding pass to Los Angeles in my hand. Instead, the words pierced my ears with the high volume of stress. We had already sat through a delay, so the announcement was met with several groans and deep sighing. To make matters worse, I had rebooked this flight after my original flight was cancelled, and after begging my husband to come to L.A. to get me, he was already on his way.

The plane had used so much gas during our holding pattern that the pilot made the sudden decision to refuel forty-five minutes before we reached our destination. It was precautionary, but since he didn't want to take any chances, Phoenix was where he decided we would land.

A few passengers (including me) started quietly protesting, "We are so close to Los Angeles, we should just keep going." As the landing gear emerged, we were aware of how much power our opinion had in directing our flight. Since that time, "Phoenix" has become my shorthand label for living out a plan that I didn't make.

When you experience this kind of script flipping in your life, you are alerted to the fact that someone else has control over your destiny. I don't remember being cognizant of our pilot until my plane was pointed toward the wrong destination, and then my eyes were riveted on the cockpit door. You have a stronger awareness of God when the script you wrote for yourself is not the one you are living. We become starkly aware that someone else is calling the shots when we're buckled into a story we didn't write.

Having our script flipped also provides us with another way to track God's presence. God becomes potentially more visible to you when the path you thought you were on starts moving a different way. As uncomfortable as that may be, "Phoenix" experiences position us for a less obstructed view of God.

Your Plan Versus the One That Happened

When we started our descent, I felt my fingers grasp the arms of my seat to steer the plane in a different direction. But during that flight I learned a lesson that stayed with me: What I did have in my power was my response.

When your plan is hijacked (which may be a poor choice of words) the only thing left is how you respond to what's happening. You can spend your energy fighting what's happening or you can look for the presence of God. When you lean in to the change and live it, you are likely to see God show up.

On a scale of one to ten, mark how you first respond when your plan is interrupted:

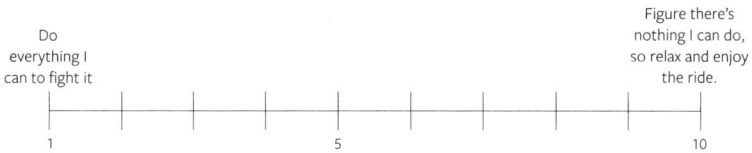

Do
everything I
can to fight it

Figure there's
nothing I can do,
so relax and enjoy
the ride.

1   5   10

Which word below best describes your emotional response when life goes off plan? (Circle one.)

angry

disappointed

scared

curious

excited

Our response to letting go of our plans has something to do with our temperament, but it also points to our faith. When life goes off plan, it's not just an opportunity to learn flexibility; it is also an invitation to trust. If you believe God is in control, there must be something in the rewrite that He has for you. Looking back, you will be able to see more clearly what it was.

Many people experienced their script flipping when Jesus arrived, and their lives were upended. Joseph experienced this at full tilt—especially when he was asked to play an unexpected role. You can only imagine the state of his heart when he discovered his fiancée was expecting a baby without his participation. Suddenly he was positioned in a new story to be a father to a child who wasn't his, and his only choice was to accept or decline this role.

This was obviously not Joseph's script for his life, but it was an opportunity for God to use him in a way he probably never imagined. When I think of Joseph's mindset at the time this was happening, I'm aware of how many things he had to let go of to embrace this plan. Relinquishing the marriage and family he'd imagined must not have been easy, not to mention the hit to his reputation. He experienced God's leading in a way many of us would envy, but the path of his life was taken completely out of his hands.

Pause here and reflect on whether you've ever started down a path you had chosen for yourself that suddenly went in a very different direction than you had planned.

What happened?

What did you have to let go of when you were redirected on this path?

Like the young couples around them, Joseph and Mary were looking toward a weeklong wedding, followed by a year of adjusting to marriage. Mary's pregnancy set them on a completely different course. After Joseph receives encouragement from an angel in a dream, he takes on the role of becoming Jesus's father and protector (Matthew 1:24). Observing how God speaks to Joseph in directing his vulnerable family (Matthew 2:13, 19) shows that Joseph's submission brought more of God's tangible presence in his life.

Have you ever felt more of God's presence when you were being led on a different path than you planned? YES / NO

If so, how?

If you think your story will go one way and it becomes something different, you have an opportunity to experience God's direction. When you are removed from the driver's seat of your life, there is more space for God to lead. Your part is no easy task: Let Him, and watch.

When a Side Story Becomes the Main Story

Buckled into the back seat of an old van, our group was being whisked from the Port-au-Prince airport to the hotel where we were staying. Around me were other speakers and pastors—Compassion International had brought us to Haiti to visit sponsored children, so we could see firsthand how their lives had changed. I had been on other trips, but this one was special because a pastor I was dating came with me. My excitement was wrapped around our relationship; I thought it would be a great way to see what we were like as a team.

The man driving our van was a pastor from Port-au-Prince named Ephraim Lindor. I was immediately captivated by his charismatic smile; even as we weaved through poverty-stricken streets, he managed to radiate joy. He'd roll down the window and wave at people, and it was obvious by the response he'd get that people loved him. Occasionally, he would stop longer to talk to someone, and I'd see him discreetly put out a bit of change in their hands. Watching Ephraim broke up the gravity of what we saw as we made our way through the itinerary of our week.

When we headed home, we had plenty of stories to fuel our future messages. But the person who stayed with me most profoundly was the pastor who drove our van. When I found out he worked for Compassion so he could pastor his church for free, I wrote him to see if there was anything I could do to support him. What I didn't know was that it would be the beginning of a twenty-five-year friendship that has changed both of our lives.

My boyfriend and I broke up soon after that trip, but Ephraim and I are still family. In the years that followed, I led several mission trips to Haiti, and people from those trips support Ephraim's ministry to this day. Ephraim prayed for years for me to find a husband, so it was poignant that I got engaged in Haiti. Unsurprisingly, my husband said God nudged him to propose on our mission trip, so I secretly suspect Ephraim's prayers were involved. Four months later, someone on the mission trip flew Ephraim to Santa Barbara to help officiate my wedding, and when I saw him beaming at the altar, I flashed on how different from the story I'd written things had turned out to be.

In my story, my pastor boyfriend and I had a lovely experience of doing team ministry. In God's story, meeting the van driver turned out to be the reason for my trip. It was just the beginning of all that was ahead.

Now it's your turn. Think back on an event that you thought was going to go one way but ended up becoming something different. It could be a trip you went on, a class you took, or a work project—anything you set out to do that had a different twist than you planned. If anything comes to mind, write down what you thought was going to happen versus the way it turned out.

Looking back, can you see any of God's orchestration in what ended up happening? If so, how?

Whether your entire life script gets flipped or just a part of it, you often get a glimpse of God in what ends up happening. It could be someone you meet because of it, something that alters your course, or possibly a change that takes place inside of you. When God flips your script, it is usually for the purpose of setting something else up to happen. But God almost always has something in it for you.

The Plans We Have for People

Another kind of script flipping is when someone comes into your life who looks or acts differently than you expected. We have pictures in our mind of who we think someone will be, and when they turn out to be different, God often uses that to reveal something to us. This is illustrated when the prophet Samuel has to find another king to serve Israel, and God helps Samuel find the one He wants anointed (1 Samuel 16). When Samuel enters Jesse's house to choose one of his sons, you can tell Samuel has an immediate idea of who it will be.

He sees Jesse's tall, muscular son Eliab and waits for God's nudge, but God is silent. In fact, Samuel does not get God's nudge on any of the sons Jesse presents. When he asks if there is anyone else he should see, Jesse's response indicates that he left his youngest son out of the lineup on purpose. Samuel asks to see him, and the Lord affirms that Jesse's son David is the one to anoint.

The Lord tells Samuel what all of us eventually come to know: We shouldn't judge people based on initial appearance (1 Samuel 16:7). What's important about a person is what is inside, and that becomes visible in time. Samuel was focused on how the king should look, but

God was focused on something much more important—the state of the future king's heart.

Has someone ever come into your life who you thought would look or act a certain way, but your script was flipped by who they turned out to be? Maybe someone you hired for a job, or ended up dating, or someone who unexpectedly became a great friend? Write down anyone who comes to mind.

Do you see evidence of God teaching you something in the surprise of who this person turned out to be? If so, what did God show you?

More often, a flipped script happens in a different way—when someone we love and care about moves in an unscripted direction. This is another opportunity to experience God, not only in what we learn, but in how we respond. A story from my six-year stint as a youth pastor memorably illustrates this truth.

I was aware of the dilemma these parents faced before they came to meet with me. Their daughter had recently made a transformation that turned their lives upside down. A year before, she had graduated from the eighth grade, a kind and gentle spirit with strawberry blond hair and freckles. In ninth grade, she came to youth group with spiked hair, a leather jacket with chains, and thick black makeup under her eyes. An aggressive personality matched her new appearance. The first time I saw her, I tried to hide my obvious shock; my students were less successful, but we all tried not to gawk at her change.

"How are you guys handling this?" I asked, fully aware that this couple's daughter had veered off their plan for parenting. They were humbled and pensive—and keenly aware of how much was riding on their response. I didn't have much to say to console them, because I wasn't sure whether this was a stage or a more permanent transformation. To this day, I have never forgotten their response.

"It's clear that the daughter we were previously parenting has left us. So we have decided our job is to love this girl until the daughter we know is in there comes back."

Instead of trying to take control of their script, these parents adjusted their part in it. They not only modeled for our youth group (and church) a beautiful lesson in parenting, but also how God can show up through us when we face an unwanted change in our script.

Sometimes we feel so invested in a person we care about that we try to step in and control what is happening. More often than not, God has a plan in what we are trying to control to do something in us.

Have you ever had someone you loved or cared for veer from the script you had for them? If so, who was it, and what did they do?

How did you respond?

Looking back, can you see God in what happened, or in what you learned from this?

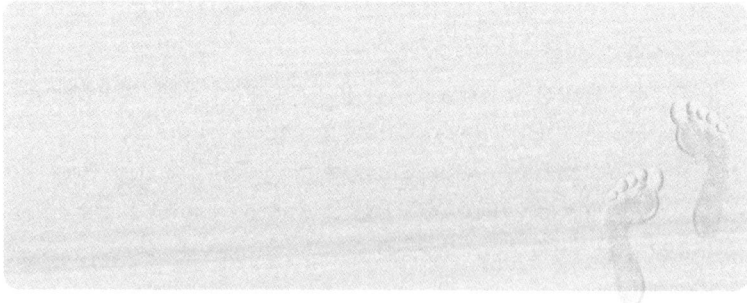

When there is a change in our script for others, it bumps up against our expectations. It can be an expectation we have for whom we will date or marry, how our friends should act, or who our children will be. The parents in the previous story learned (and modeled) a huge lesson in responding to a changed script when their daughter showed up with a drastically different attitude and appearance. Sometimes a script gets flipped on what we expect someone else to be in order to show us who we need to become.

When things don't go the way you intended, God often emerges in what happens. There are also times when something you hoped would happen is changed because of a greater plan that will live on after you. When things aren't going the way you thought they would, there might be something bigger that God is orchestrating. One of our greatest glimpses of God is when we see how this orchestration turns out.

The Plan Around Your Plan

When something we thought would happen turns out to be different, it often turns out to be a lot bigger. We can't always see what's happening when we are living it, but we see more of what God did when we look back.

Paul wrote many letters to churches while sitting in prison, but I'm guessing he was frustrated, thinking that he could have a bigger impact if he was seeing them. If he could visit the churches in person, he could encourage people face-to-face, rather than putting his encouragement in written form. What Paul couldn't see was what

God was going to end up doing with the letters he was writing. We often have to trust that what we don't see is space that God holds.

When my husband, Jere, and I were in Corinth filming a study on 1 Corinthians 13, we were saddened to discover the relatively short impact of Paul's ministry on the church in Corinth. The church suffered many conflicts—and when you read the Corinthian letters, you can pick up Paul's tone of frustration that his instruction wasn't being lived out. So many things he taught them weren't remembered after he left them, and that's why he was so disheartened in instructing them. When Jere and I learned that the church in Corinth was still struggling with the same issues a hundred years after Paul's lifetime, it was clear the fruit of his ministry there was not what Paul had hoped.

But what *is* amazing is that now, in the twenty-first century, these Corinthian letters from Paul are so significant that my husband and I traveled to Corinth to film this study. Words in these letters not only became part of the New Testament, but they have shaped and impacted billions of believers to this day. Even nonbelievers have heard words from 1 Corinthians 13 in countless wedding ceremonies they've attended. The receptivity to Paul's teachings in Corinth may have been disappointing at that time, but they ended up being part of a script God was writing that would outlive anything Paul imagined for what he wrote.

When I stood in Corinth, I thought about what God did with Paul's ministry to the Corinthians. What ended up happening to his letters was probably vastly different from—and far greater than—what Paul thought their impact would be. All the letters Paul wrote were intended for far smaller audiences than the audiences who ended up reading them. How ironic that the letters Paul wrote to churches *between* his missionary journeys ended up being his ministry's furthest reach.

As you think back on your life so far, has anything you've done turned into something bigger or different than you thought it would be? Maybe you ended up impacting more (or different) people than you expected, or what you did ended up having a different purpose than you originally thought?

If anything comes to mind, write it here.

In what ways do you see God's purpose in flipping the script on what you thought you were doing or in what ended up happening?

When we look back on things we've done, it's interesting to dream forward to what God might do with them. When we've ended up somewhere we didn't plan to be, or doing something we never intended to do, what eventually happens because of that could be bigger than we think.

The ultimate script flip is found in Paul's words when he closes out his second letter to the Corinthians. Referring to Jesus, he says, "He was crucified in weakness, yet he lives by God's power"

(2 Corinthians 13:4). What looked at the time of Jesus's death to be a small, sad end to a hopeful ministry turned into a different story when Jesus was resurrected. Paul's letters went through a similar transition after the Corinthian church died, when the letters became something much bigger than Paul could have dreamed.

When my husband and I finished reading the plaque documenting the dismal history of the Corinthian church, we realized that we weren't reading the full story as we looked at the Bible in our hands.

── ── ── ── ── ── ── ── **Moving Forward** ── ── ── ── ── ── ── ── ──

So how do we learn to lean into a changed script knowing God is at work in ways we might not be able to imagine? It means relinquishing the way we think things should be, in order to trust there is some reason for the way things are. Looking back on how God moved in unexpected ways in the past, we gain confidence and hope for when change happens in the future. The goal is to recognize *in the moment* that God is doing something in, around, or beyond us because of this change that we will eventually see.

When we think something we're doing is going to turn out one way, we must hold it loosely enough that God can adjust it without our clinging. Instead of focusing on what's not happening the way you want it to happen, look for what *is* happening instead. Living with a looser grip allows God greater space to be the Pilot. And when we look for what God is doing or teaching us, we begin to see God more.

So, here's your exercise moving forward: The next time your script gets flipped, try to let go of your agenda. Instead of staying frustrated that something is not happening that you wanted to happen, lean in and live. Observe the people around you and what is happening inside you. Use the space below to write about your experience and how it felt. Then come back to this page three months from now, and as you look back on what you wrote down, take note of anything that has transpired because of what happened.

Make a mark in your calendar and come back to this page in three months, and as you look back on what you wrote down, take note of anything that has transpired in your life since this "script flip" happened.

Three-month review:

When you look back and see more of what God was doing, the God of the rearview mirror will invite you to a greater trust at the time He works.

eight

The Thirty-Thousand-Foot View

The phrase *thirty-thousand-foot view* is used to invite people to pull back to see the big picture. It originates from the view you have when you are on an airplane and watch what happens to the ground as you ascend. The higher you get, the more you see the bigger picture of where you were.

When I imagine God's view of our lives, I think of it with this perspective. God not only sees who we are, but also who will come after us, and how we fit in. He sees the scope of our life, including all that will happen after our life is finished. Contemplating this perspective not only gives us hope for what our life may mean, but also fills us with courage and intention for the days we have.

Unless you pull back to notice all that happens around your story, you miss some of the nuances of what God is doing. Piecing it all together also involves watching for God's activity as you continue to walk through life. This is what the Israelites did when they made stone pile altars along the roads where they lived and traveled. When they encountered God, these piles of stones were commemorative altars that they (and others before them) built. Revisiting these piles would help them gain courage for what was currently happening, as well as any fear they had for what lay ahead of them. This perspective of God's trustworthiness was achieved not by going up in an airplane, but by traveling on foot between these piles of stones.

The preceding chapters have been an invitation to see God at work by learning seven ways to track His presence. This final chapter invites you to see the thirty-thousand-foot (stone-pile) view of the ways God has shown up in your life. Pulling back to see evidence of God in your life so far brings you more assurance that you'll see God in the future. It also helps you see that some things you are living right now may be viewed differently when you look back.

For this thirty-thousand-foot, stone-pile view, you are going to choose one way that you saw evidence of God's presence from each of the preceding chapters. You can either go through them on your own and choose one piece of evidence from each chapter that is most meaningful to you, or if you want some direction in selecting them, here is some help:

From chapter 1, choose the first time you had a God awareness, or had a strong sense of God's presence.

From chapter 2, choose when you most clearly heard from God.

From chapter 3, choose a time when a door to something you wanted closed in order for something that ended up better to happen.

From chapter 4, choose the story of some coincidence or timing from your life that most clearly revealed the hand of God.

From chapter 5, choose a mirror God brought to you that moved you toward growth AND a cliff God brought you to so He could show you His presence in your inadequacy.

From chapter 6, choose a thorn (or a pain) you had to endure that helped you see God in the way it was used.

From chapter 7, choose the script flip you are most grateful for now because of what it brought to your life.

On the next page is an illustration of eight stones in a pile. Choose a word or phrase to symbolize each of the eight ways you saw God work from the list above. (Remember, chapter 5 has two.) Write that word or phrase in each of the stones in the pile.

This page will be your thirty-thousand-foot view to remember God's presence and faithfulness to you. It's your stone pile of the tangible ways God has worked in your life. Put a marker in this page—it is where you'll turn to get a scope of God's faithfulness by remembering all the different ways He has shown up.

The word *remember* is so important that it is used over two hundred times in the Bible. God knows that it is in our looking back that we find confidence to trust Him for what is ahead. Remembering God's faithfulness enables you (like the Israelites) to hold on to Him. The different ways you've learned to see God's presence in your past will help you know where to look for what God might be doing right now.

Here are four last insights to remember as you track God from here on out.

Stay in the Story

We often leave our stories when we come to a satisfying ending—and we miss out on what happens as the story continues. When we keep our eye on our stories, we get to see what happens as they evolve.

Years ago, I volunteered with kids in an afterschool program in Los Angeles, in an area where homelessness was rampant. At that time, God brought me to an eleven-year-old girl who became a precious gift to my life. Like many of the girls around her, she became pregnant as a teenager, but unlike her friends, she decided she wanted to give her baby up for adoption. After we poured through adoption books, the couple she had carefully chosen ended up falling through the day her baby was born. Days later, I was with my best friend in Orange County, and she happened to tell me about a couple who taught at her kids' school who were struggling with conceiving and desperately wanted a child.

Through a miraculous convergence of timing and circumstances, I connected with this couple, and they wanted to hear more about this baby. After an exuberant meeting, my girl chose them to be the parents of her baby boy. A few weeks after the adoption was finalized, I attended a baby shower and watched the women who knew this couple passing the baby around the room, thrilled to see their prayers answered. I knew I was witnessing God's miraculous intervention in this baby's life.

Fast-forward seventeen years: Because of their experience, this couple had adopted two more boys born to inner-city teenage mothers. They sent me a Christmas card of their family, and an updated photo of the baby I had helped place into their arms. He was signing a full-ride basketball scholarship to a Christian university with his parents beaming behind him. By staying in the story, I witnessed the incredible evolution of God's work.

As I continue to age, I realize how important it is to stay in our stories. We tend to leave things that happen behind us when we move on in our life. But some of the best glimpses of God come from tracking what continues to happen in our past stories. Mining the people and places that have been part of our faith journey, we find more evidence of His work.

So take a moment and choose one of the faith stories of your past that you might be able to revisit to find out what has happened. You can choose a story from your pile of stones or something from a previous chapter in this book. If you are able to follow up and see how the story has evolved, write down what has happened since.

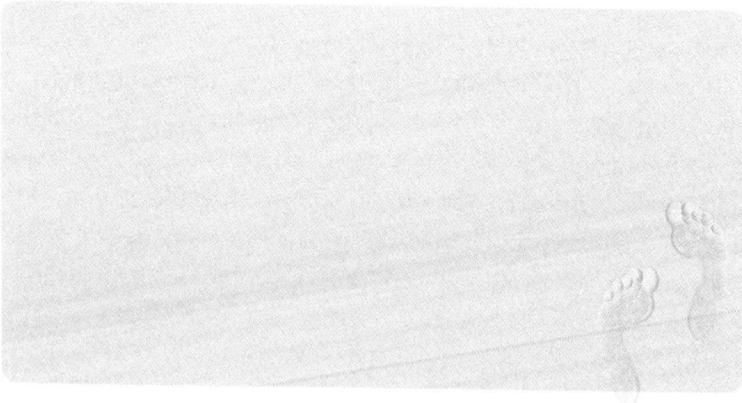

Let this exercise serve as a beginning practice of what you will keep on doing with your faith stories. Tracking what continues to happen in them may reveal more signs of God's work.

See the Connections

God doesn't just work one way at a time; He works different ways all the time. When you see how one story connects with another story, and how sometimes a third story comes from it, you get a more expansive view of God's work. It takes some deeper reflecting to see these connections, but it's worth the work for your faith.

Four months after my broken engagement, when I got the call to work in a church, it moved me into a future that rewrote my heartbreak. But I didn't realize then that my broken engagement would be strategic in the future of my stepson's life. My ex-fiancé was a marine reservist, and while he was deployed during our engagement, the chaplain introduced me to a military wife named Melissa. We became friends, and after my engagement ended, she stayed in my life.

Melissa was in a family of marines—her husband, son, and father-in-law all served our country. She and her husband became even closer friends when I married my husband, and we attended various military ceremonies, never realizing the influence they were having on our boy's life. When he decided to become a marine, he said it was their influence that drew him to it. Watching him become what my ex-fiancé had been, I realized the thirty-thousand-foot view of this story made it more unimaginable than I thought.

My story with Ephraim has also evolved into new chapters through different connections. He was with me years ago when I met my

Compassion child from Haiti, and helped translate so she and I could talk. After twelve years of sponsorship, she had to drop out of school to work for her family, and we lost touch when she left the Compassion program. Years later, I got a message from her on Facebook, and not only was she now a young woman with two children, she posted a picture of herself in a cap and gown, so I wondered if she had gone back to school.

Because she spoke only Creole, I was unable to ask her about her life since our sponsorship ended. So I wrote to Ephraim and connected the two of them, and was then able to learn through him all that happened since my sponsorship stopped. She had gone back to school and gotten certified in cosmetology, but with all the problems in Haiti, her children's father lost his employment. Because of their situation, she couldn't get the supplies she needed for the job she was certified to do. Ephraim and I were able to pool some of our resources to supply her business, so I had the opportunity for another chapter in my support to her. God added to the story of my Compassion child by connecting it with the story of my ongoing friendship with Ephraim, eight years after my sponsorship stopped.

Both these new stories came from my original stories of being engaged to the wrong guy and meeting the van driver during our trip to Haiti. It's strange to think that if those original events hadn't happened, I never would have experienced God's weaving of these threads.

As you think back, can you see a story that has emerged from another one of your stories? If any connection comes to mind, write it here.

If you need more prodding, can you think of anyone you met through a story in your past who became significant to you later? Or something that happened down the line because of a story that didn't turn out the way you hoped? If so, write about it.

When you peel back to see the thirty-thousand-foot view of how God works, you'll be amazed to see how God weaves together different parts of your stories. As you take the time to see the connections, you'll have a more expansive view of the way the Artist works.

Reflect Regularly

Without pausing to reflect, we can miss a lot of what God is doing. But we have to create space in our lives in order to look back. The word *remember* is not just a directive, it's also an invitation—to get a view of God's work that we don't see while we are living it. We see so much more of what God was doing in our lives when we carve out some time to look back.

This is part of the reason the Israelites made their stone piles—so they could remember all God had done for them. I imagine that when people passed those stone altars years after they were constructed, it gave their faith a boost. It helped them remember God was at work—especially when they couldn't see it in their lives at the time.

Setting aside time to reflect helps you experience what the Israelites did when they revisited their stone altars. Life moved at a much slower pace then, partly because people walked wherever they went. While many things have changed, what hasn't changed is our need to reflect on things that have happened to us. Without this reflection, we miss the many ways God shows up.

Author John Mark Comer and other spiritual leaders have brought back the ancient practice of Sabbath, which is essentially a time-out to enjoy God and sit in His presence. In Comer's book, *The Ruthless Elimination of Hurry*, he describes how to create this space.

To begin, you set aside a day. Clear your schedule. TURN OFF YOUR PHONE. Say a prayer to invite the Holy Spirit to pastor you into his presence. And then? *Rest* and *worship*. In whatever way is life giving for your soul.[1]

Traditionally, the Sabbath is a twenty-four-hour period each week, but the purpose of Sabbath is to stop and reflect on God's presence. It is a regular rhythm in our week that allows us to reconnect ourselves to the story God is writing with our lives. Without taking time for this reflection, we become human doings, rather than human beings who see how God is working within us and around us. We can't track God without taking time to notice what God is doing, and that practice of reflection is part of what fuels our faith.

If this is something you want to incorporate into your schedule, take a moment and think about when you can set aside time to start regularly reflecting. Find one way you can continue tracking God after you finish this book—a time you will set aside to be with and hear from God. Write down when you will do this and where you will do it. Putting it in your schedule will help you follow through.

A last word of encouragement about reflection is from one of my literary mentors, Philip Yancey, who wrote a little book called

Finding God in Unexpected Places. He wrote two books that received Christian Book of the Year awards, but this lesser-known book fueled some of his thoughts. In it, Yancey writes these words about taking time to reflect on God:

> It takes great effort, and considerable faith, to keep the Big Picture in mind. In some ways it makes me feel utterly insignificant, in some ways eternally significant. If the God who engineered creation with such precision professes some whit of interest in what takes place on this speck of a planet, the least I can do is wander away from the streetlights more often and look up.[2]

Whatever it means for you to "wander away from the streetlights," find some time in your schedule to do it. By taking time away from the distractions, we see more of God in our life.

Leave Room for Surprises

This final insight into tracking God is may be the hardest to practice. Most of us love surprises when they happen—what's hard is waiting expectantly for what you do not know. Because surprises, by definition, happen when you're not expecting them, you have to learn to wait in anticipation when things look dark and nothing is happening. Holding space for God to surprise you is a discipline—especially when God is silent, and disappointment or doubt threatens your soul.

It was the middle of a dark time that caused me to develop what I now feed on when I'm trying to stay hopeful. I was speaking at a conference, and I took the risk of sharing the story of my broken engagement before I had any idea it would be resolved. When I got to the end, something boiled up in me at the moment I was groping for some kind of hopeful transition. I looked out to the sea of forlorn faces and said, "I don't know what's going to happen, but I got up this morning, so as bad as this story looks, God's not through." Somehow, my declaration of hope in the middle of the story seemed to help people feel encouraged about their own unmet longings. Our middle-of-the-story testimonies give people strength to hold onto their faith.

At one time or another, all of us live in the middle of the story. In some part of our lives, we can't yet see what God is going to do. There are different ways to live in this space—we can try to force the ending we want and attempt to live what we want to happen. Or we can sit hopefully in the darkness and leave room for what God will do.

The best stories in my life have come out of pain and loss and grave disappointment. We were made to have our souls thrilled by resurrection, so it makes sense that the most powerful manifestation of God comes through loss. But holding space for that thrill is our lifelong challenge. Even when we've seen God come through before, we lose our hope that it will happen again when a dream or desire is lost. That's when we need the grit, perseverance, and dogged faith of middle-of-the story theology—to know God will give us what we need and take us through.

The best prophet to go to for help with this is Habakkuk, who, despite his hard-to-say name, models for us how to leave room for surprises. The reason I love his book in the Bible is because it ends with no more resolve than it begins. Habakkuk is still waiting for God to show up all the way up to—and through—his ending. Near the end of his book, he speaks of looking confidently for what he can't yet see that God will do. His middle-of-the-story testimony inspires us to hold on in the unknown parts of our life:

> Though the olive crop fails
>   and the fields produce no food,
> though there are no sheep in the pen
>   and no cattle in the stalls,
> yet I will rejoice in the LORD,
>   I will be joyful in God my Savior.
>   Habakkuk 3:17–18

After these words of hope for what hasn't happened yet, Habakkuk offers us insight about what he's relying on while he is waiting. Here's what he says will help him have the strength to make it through:

> The Sovereign LORD is my strength;
>   he makes my feet like the feet of a deer,
>   he enables me to tread on the heights.
>   Habakkuk 3:19

In seasons when can't see what's ahead, God positions us to receive what only these seasons can give us. We are led to the heights to wait for the big picture to unfold, while we experience, in real time, God's ongoing help. Perhaps that is another one of God's surprises—that through His power we are able to live one more day trusting. When we look back, we realize that by enduring these seasons, we did something we didn't know we had the strength to do.

Tracking God builds your faith muscle so you can move forward with confidence that God is with you. Every glimpse of God you've written down propels you to move forward with trust. Because you've learned to see God's presence in the story you've lived, you now know how to find God in the story you're living. And if there is only one thing you remember, let it be this: If you're still breathing, no matter how it looks, your story isn't through.

Acknowledgments

This book is special to me because it belongs to the reader. For that reason, I want to acknowledge YOU. Thank you for choosing to pick up this book—I believe it will unlock some treasures from God in your life.

I also want to acknowledge the people at Bethany House Publishers who loved this idea the moment they saw it, and especially Jeff Braun, who championed it.

And finally, to my husband, Jere, ministry partner Melissa, and all the people who've done my books and studies or watched me speak, you've done enough listening to my story; now it's time to tell yours.

Notes

Chapter 1 Footprints

1. There are several versions of the "Footprints in the Sand" poem, and although it is widely reported as having been written by Mary Stevenson in 1936, there are at least three other people who claim authorship. (See Rachel Aviv, "Enter Sandman: Who Wrote 'Footprints'?," *Poetry Foundation*, March 19, 2008, https://www.poetryfoundation.org/articles/68974/enter-sandman.)

2. This summary of "Footprints in the Sand" is based on the version found on a bookmark with no author identified.

3. The comic strip (likely derived or adapted from Kris Straub, *Chainsawsuit*, August 8, 2012, https://chainsawsuit.krisstraub.com/20120808.shtml) was posted on Leslie Scoopmire, "Second Chances, Kicking and Screaming: Speaking to the Soul," *Abiding in Hope* (blog), March 17, 2022.

Chapter 2 Hearing God

1. Pete Greig, *How to Hear God: A Simple Guide for Normal People* (Zondervan, 2022), 3.

2. Jacob Firet, *Dynamics in Pastoring* (Eerdmans, 1986), 99–116.

Chapter 5 Mirrors and Cliffs

1. Richard Rohr, *Breathing Under Water: Spirituality and the Twelve Steps* (Franciscan Media, 2011), 31.

Chapter 6 Power in Weakness

1. C. S. Lewis, *The Problem of Pain* (HarperCollins, 2001), 92.

Chapter 8 The Thirty-Thousand-Foot View

1. John Mark Comer, *The Ruthless Elimination of Hurry* (WaterBrook, 2019), 174.

2. Philip Yancey, *Finding God in Unexpected Places* (Ballantine, 1995), 25.

LAURIE POLICH SHORT is a popular speaker, author, and part of the teaching team at Oceanhills Covenant Church in Santa Barbara, California. A graduate of Fuller Theological Seminary, Laurie has spoken to more than 500,000 people at conferences, colleges, churches, and denominational events around the country, and she has been featured on RightNow Media, *Life Today*, PBS, *Focus on the Family*, and more. Find Laurie's videos and studies at LaurieShort.com.

Connect with Laurie:

LaurieShort.com

@LauriePShort

Laurie P Short